TEST PREPARATION

FTCE

Middle Grades Mathematics 5-9
Secrets Study Guide
Part 2 of 2

DEAR FUTURE EXAM SUCCESS STORY

First of all, **THANK YOU** for purchasing Mometrix study materials!

Second, congratulations! You are one of the few determined test-takers who are committed to doing whatever it takes to excel on your exam. **You have come to the right place.** We developed these study materials with one goal in mind: to deliver you the information you need in a format that's concise and easy to use.

In addition to optimizing your guide for the content of the test, we've outlined our recommended steps for breaking down the preparation process into small, attainable goals so you can make sure you stay on track.

We've also analyzed the entire test-taking process, identifying the most common pitfalls and showing how you can overcome them and be ready for any curveball the test throws you.

Standardized testing is one of the biggest obstacles on your road to success, which only increases the importance of doing well in the high-pressure, high-stakes environment of test day. Your results on this test could have a significant impact on your future, and this guide provides the information and practical advice to help you achieve your full potential on test day.

Your success is our success

We would love to hear from you! If you would like to share the story of your exam success or if you have any questions or comments in regard to our products, please contact us at **800-673-8175** or **support@mometrix.com**.

Thanks again for your business and we wish you continued success!

Sincerely,
The Mometrix Test Preparation Team

> **Need more help? Check out our flashcards at:**
> **http://MometrixFlashcards.com/FTCE**

TABLE OF CONTENTS

Geometry and Measurement and Spatial Sense

Measurement Principles

PRECISION, ACCURACY, AND ERROR

Precision: How reliable and repeatable a measurement is. The more consistent the data is with repeated testing, the more precise it is. For example, hitting a target consistently in the same spot, which may or may not be the center of the target, is precision.

Accuracy: How close the data is to the correct data. For example, hitting a target consistently in the center area of the target, whether or not the hits are all in the same spot, is accuracy.

Note: it is possible for data to be precise without being accurate. If a scale is off balance, the data will be precise, but will not be accurate. For data to have precision and accuracy, it must be repeatable and correct.

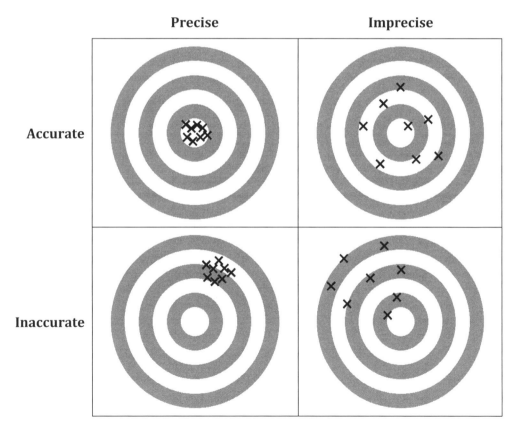

Approximate error: The amount of error in a physical measurement. Approximate error is often reported as the measurement, followed by the ± symbol and the amount of the approximate error.

Maximum possible error: Half the magnitude of the smallest unit used in the measurement. For example, if the unit of measurement is 1 centimeter, the maximum possible error is $\frac{1}{2}$ cm, written as

1

±0.5 cm following the measurement. It is important to apply significant figures in reporting maximum possible error. Do not make the answer appear more accurate than the least accurate of your measurements.

ROUNDING AND ESTIMATION

Rounding is reducing the digits in a number while still trying to keep the value similar. The result will be less accurate, but it will be in a simpler form and will be easier to use. Whole numbers can be rounded to the nearest ten, hundred or thousand.

When you are asked to estimate the solution to a problem, you will need to provide only an approximate figure or **estimation** for your answer. In this situation, you will need to round each number in the calculation to the level indicated (nearest hundred, nearest thousand, etc.) or to a level that makes sense for the numbers involved. When estimating a sum **all numbers must be rounded to the same level**. You cannot round one number to the nearest thousand while rounding another to the nearest hundred.

> **Review Video: Rounding and Estimation**
> Visit mometrix.com/academy and enter code: 126243

SCIENTIFIC NOTATION

Scientific notation is a way of writing large numbers in a shorter form. The form $a \times 10^n$ is used in scientific notation, where a is greater than or equal to 1, but less than 10, and n is the number of places the decimal must move to get from the original number to a. Example: The number 230,400,000 is cumbersome to write. To write the value in scientific notation, place a decimal point between the first and second numbers, and include all digits through the last non-zero digit ($a = 2.304$). To find the appropriate power of 10, count the number of places the decimal point had to move ($n = 8$). The number is positive if the decimal moved to the left, and negative if it moved to the right. We can then write 230,400,000 as 2.304×10^8. If we look instead at the number 0.00002304, we have the same value for a, but this time the decimal moved 5 places to the right ($n = -5$). Thus, 0.00002304 can be written as 2.304×10^{-5}. Using this notation makes it simple to compare very large or very small numbers. By comparing exponents, it is easy to see that 3.28×10^4 is smaller than 1.51×10^5, because 4 is less than 5.

> **Review Video: Scientific Notation**
> Visit mometrix.com/academy and enter code: 976454

PRACTICE

P1. Round each number to the indicated degree:

   (a) Round to the nearest ten: 11; 47; 118

   (b) Round to the nearest hundred: 78; 980; 248

   (c) Round each number to the nearest thousand: 302; 1274; 3756

P2. Estimate the solution to 345,932 + 96,369 by rounding each number to the nearest ten thousand.

P3. A runner's heart beats 422 times over the course of six minutes. About how many times did the runner's heart beat during each minute?

PRACTICE SOLUTIONS

P1. (a) When rounding to the nearest ten, anything ending in 5 or greater rounds up. So, 11 rounds to 10, 47 rounds to 50, and 118 rounds to 120.

(b) When rounding to the nearest hundred, anything ending in 50 or greater rounds up. So, 78 rounds to 100, 980 rounds to 1000, and 248 rounds to 200.

(c) When rounding to the nearest thousand, anything ending in 500 or greater rounds up. So, 302 rounds to 0, 1274 rounds to 1000, and 3756 rounds to 4000.

P2. Start by rounding each number to the nearest ten thousand: 345,932 becomes 350,000, and 96,369 becomes 100,000. Then, add the rounded numbers: 350,000 + 100,000 = 450,000. So, the answer is approximately 450,000. The exact answer would be 345,932 + 96,369 = 442,301. So, the estimate of 450,000 is a similar value to the exact answer.

P3. "About how many" indicates that you need to estimate the solution. In this case, look at the numbers you are given. 422 can be rounded down to 420, which is easily divisible by 6. A good estimate is 420 ÷ 6 = 70 beats per minute. More accurately, the patient's heart rate was just over 70 beats per minute since his heart actually beat a little more than 420 times in six minutes.

Units of Measurement

METRIC MEASUREMENT PREFIXES

Giga-: one billion (1 *giga*watt is one billion watts)
Mega-: one million (1 *mega*hertz is one million hertz)
Kilo-: one thousand (1 *kilo*gram is one thousand grams)
Deci-: one tenth (1 *deci*meter is one tenth of a meter)
Centi-: one hundredth (1 *centi*meter is one hundredth of a meter)
Milli-: one thousandth (1 *milli*liter is one thousandth of a liter)
Micro-: one millionth (1 *micro*gram is one millionth of a gram)

MEASUREMENT CONVERSION

When converting between units, the goal is to maintain the same meaning but change the way it is displayed. In order to go from a larger unit to a smaller unit, multiply the number of the known amount by the equivalent amount. When going from a smaller unit to a larger unit, divide the number of the known amount by the equivalent amount.

For complicated conversions, it may be helpful to set up conversion fractions. In these fractions, one fraction is the **conversion factor**. The other fraction has the unknown amount in the numerator. So, the known value is placed in the denominator. Sometimes the second fraction has the known value from the problem in the numerator, and the unknown in the denominator. Multiply the two fractions to get the converted measurement. Note that since the numerator and the denominator of the factor are equivalent, the value of the fraction is 1. That is why we can say that the result in the new units is equal to the result in the old units even though they have different numbers.

It can often be necessary to chain known conversion factors together. As an example, consider converting 512 square inches to square meters. We know that there are 2.54 centimeters in an inch and 100 centimeters in a meter, and that we will need to square each of these factors to achieve the conversion we are looking for.

3

$$\frac{512 \text{ in}^2}{1} \times \left(\frac{2.54 \text{ cm}}{1 \text{ in}}\right)^2 \times \left(\frac{1 \text{ m}}{100 \text{ cm}}\right)^2 = \frac{512 \text{ in}^2}{1} \times \left(\frac{6.4516 \text{ cm}^2}{1 \text{ in}^2}\right) \times \left(\frac{1 \text{ m}^2}{10000 \text{ cm}^2}\right) = 0.330 \text{ m}^2$$

COMMON UNITS AND EQUIVALENTS

METRIC EQUIVALENTS

1000 µg (microgram)	1 mg
1000 mg (milligram)	1 g
1000 g (gram)	1 kg
1000 kg (kilogram)	1 metric ton
1000 mL (milliliter)	1 L
1000 µm (micrometer)	1 mm
1000 mm (millimeter)	1 m
100 cm (centimeter)	1 m
1000 m (meter)	1 km

DISTANCE AND AREA MEASUREMENT

Unit	Abbreviation	U.S. equivalent	Metric equivalent
Inch	in	1 inch	2.54 centimeters
Foot	ft	12 inches	0.305 meters
Yard	yd	3 feet	0.914 meters
Mile	mi	5280 feet	1.609 kilometers
Acre	ac	4840 square yards	0.405 hectares
Square Mile	mi^2	640 acres	2.590 square kilometers

CAPACITY MEASUREMENTS

Unit	Abbreviation	U.S. equivalent	Metric equivalent
Fluid Ounce	fl oz	8 fluid drams	29.573 milliliters
Cup	cp	8 fluid ounces	0.237 liter
Pint	pt	16 fluid ounces	0.473 liter
Quart	qt	2 pints	0.946 liter
Gallon	gal	4 quarts	3.785 liters
Teaspoon	t or tsp	1 fluid dram	5 milliliters
Tablespoon	T or tbsp	4 fluid drams	15 or 16 milliliters
Cubic Centimeter	cc or cm^3	0.271 drams	1 milliliter

WEIGHT MEASUREMENTS

Unit	Abbreviation	U.S. equivalent	Metric equivalent
Ounce	oz	16 drams	28.35 grams
Pound	lb	16 ounces	453.6 grams
Ton	t	2,000 pounds	907.2 kilograms

VOLUME AND WEIGHT MEASUREMENT CLARIFICATIONS

Always be careful when using ounces and fluid ounces. They are not equivalent.

1 pint = 16 fluid ounces   1 fluid ounce ≠ 1 ounce
1 pound = 16 ounces   1 pint ≠ 1 pound

Having one pint of something does not mean you have one pound of it. In the same way, just because something weighs one pound does not mean that its volume is one pint.

In the United States, the word "ton" by itself refers to a short ton or a net ton. Do not confuse this with a long ton (also called a gross ton) or a metric ton (also spelled *tonne*), which have different measurement equivalents.

$$1 \text{ U.S. ton} = 2000 \text{ pounds} \qquad \neq \qquad 1 \text{ metric ton} = 1000 \text{ kilograms}$$

PRACTICE

P1. Perform the following conversions:

(a) 1.4 meters to centimeters

(b) 218 centimeters to meters

(c) 42 inches to feet

(d) 15 kilograms to pounds

(e) 80 ounces to pounds

(f) 2 miles to kilometers

(g) 5 feet to centimeters

(h) 15.14 liters to gallons

(i) 8 quarts to liters

(j) 13.2 pounds to grams

PRACTICE SOLUTIONS

P1. (a) $\frac{100 \text{ cm}}{1 \text{ m}} = \frac{x \text{ cm}}{1.4 \text{ m}}$ Cross multiply to get $x = 140$

(b) $\frac{100 \text{ cm}}{1 \text{ m}} = \frac{218 \text{ cm}}{x \text{ m}}$ Cross multiply to get $100x = 218$, or $x = 2.18$

(c) $\frac{12 \text{ in}}{1 \text{ ft}} = \frac{42 \text{ in}}{x \text{ ft}}$ Cross multiply to get $12x = 42$, or $x = 3.5$

(d) $15 \text{ kilograms } \times \frac{2.2 \text{ pounds}}{1 \text{ kilogram}} = 33 \text{ pounds}$

(e) $80 \text{ ounces } \times \frac{1 \text{ pound}}{16 \text{ ounces}} = 5 \text{ pounds}$

(f) $2 \text{ miles } \times \frac{1.609 \text{ kilometers}}{1 \text{ mile}} = 3.218 \text{ kilometers}$

(g) $5 \text{ feet } \times \frac{12 \text{ inches}}{1 \text{ foot}} \times \frac{2.54 \text{ centimeters}}{1 \text{ inch}} = 152.4 \text{ centimeters}$

(h) $15.14 \text{ liters } \times \frac{1 \text{ gallon}}{3.785 \text{ liters}} = 4 \text{ gallons}$

5

(i) 8 quarts $\times \frac{1\text{ gallon}}{4\text{ quarts}} \times \frac{3.785\text{ liters}}{1\text{ gallon}} = 7.57$ liters

(j) 13.2 pounds $\times \frac{1\text{ kilogram}}{2.2\text{ pounds}} \times \frac{1000\text{ grams}}{1\text{ kilogram}} = 6000$ grams

Lines and Planes

POINTS AND LINES

A **point** is a fixed location in space, has no size or dimensions, and is commonly represented by a dot. A **line** is a set of points that extends infinitely in two opposite directions. It has length, but no width or depth. A line can be defined by any two distinct points that it contains. A **line segment** is a portion of a line that has definite endpoints. A **ray** is a portion of a line that extends from a single point on that line in one direction along the line. It has a definite beginning, but no ending.

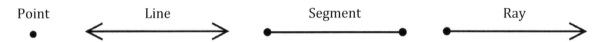

INTERACTIONS BETWEEN LINES

Intersecting lines are lines that have exactly one point in common. **Concurrent lines** are multiple lines that intersect at a single point. **Perpendicular lines** are lines that intersect at right angles. They are represented by the symbol ⊥. The shortest distance from a line to a point not on the line is a perpendicular segment from the point to the line. **Parallel lines** are lines in the same plane that have no points in common and never meet. It is possible for lines to be in different planes, have no points in common, and never meet, but they are not parallel because they are in different planes.

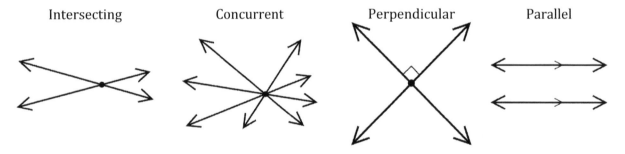

A **transversal** is a line that intersects at least two other lines, which may or may not be parallel to one another. A transversal that intersects parallel lines is a common occurrence in geometry. A **bisector** is a line or line segment that divides another line segment into two equal lengths. A **perpendicular bisector** of a line segment is composed of points that are equidistant from the endpoints of the segment it is dividing.

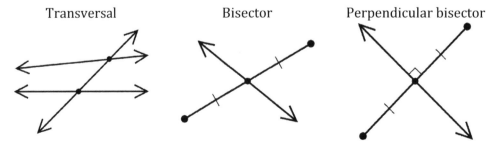

The **projection of a point on a line** is the point at which a perpendicular line drawn from the given point to the given line intersects the line. This is also the shortest distance from the given point to the line. The **projection of a segment on a line** is a segment whose endpoints are the points formed when perpendicular lines are drawn from the endpoints of the given segment to the given line. This is similar to the length a diagonal line appears to be when viewed from above.

Projection of a point on a line   Projection of a segment on a line

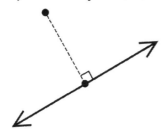 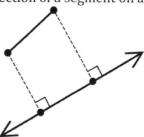

PLANES

A **plane** is a two-dimensional flat surface defined by three non-collinear points. A plane extends an infinite distance in all directions in those two dimensions. It contains an infinite number of points, parallel lines and segments, intersecting lines and segments, as well as parallel or intersecting rays. A plane will never contain a three-dimensional figure or skew lines, lines that don't intersect and are not parallel. Two given planes are either parallel or they intersect at a line. A plane may intersect a circular conic surface to form **conic sections**, such as a parabola, hyperbola, circle or ellipse.

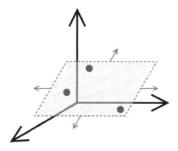

Review Video: Lines and Planes
Visit mometrix.com/academy and enter code: 554267

Angles

ANGLES AND VERTICES

An **angle** is formed when two lines or line segments meet at a common point. It may be a common starting point for a pair of segments or rays, or it may be the intersection of lines. Angles are represented by the symbol ∠.

The **vertex** is the point at which two segments or rays meet to form an angle. If the angle is formed by intersecting rays, lines, and/or line segments, the vertex is the point at which four angles are

formed. The pairs of angles opposite one another are called vertical angles, and their measures are equal.

- An **acute** angle is an angle with a degree measure less than 90°.
- A **right** angle is an angle with a degree measure of exactly 90°.
- An **obtuse** angle is an angle with a degree measure greater than 90° but less than 180°.
- A **straight angle** is an angle with a degree measure of exactly 180°. This is also a semicircle.
- A **reflex angle** is an angle with a degree measure greater than 180° but less than 360°.
- A **full angle** is an angle with a degree measure of exactly 360°.

RELATIONSHIPS BETWEEN ANGLES

Two angles whose sum is exactly 90° are said to be **complementary**. The two angles may or may not be adjacent. In a right triangle, the two acute angles are complementary.

Two angles whose sum is exactly 180° are said to be **supplementary**. The two angles may or may not be adjacent. Two intersecting lines always form two pairs of supplementary angles. Adjacent supplementary angles will always form a straight line.

Two angles that have the same vertex and share a side are said to be **adjacent**. Vertical angles are not adjacent because they share a vertex but no common side.

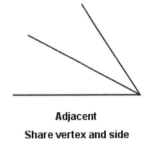

Adjacent
Share vertex and side

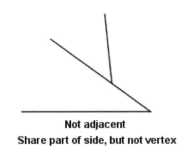

Not adjacent
Share part of side, but not vertex

When two parallel lines are cut by a transversal, the angles that are between the two parallel lines are **interior angles**. In the diagram below, angles 3, 4, 5, and 6 are interior angles.

When two parallel lines are cut by a transversal, the angles that are outside the parallel lines are **exterior angles**. In the diagram below, angles 1, 2, 7, and 8 are exterior angles.

When two parallel lines are cut by a transversal, the angles that are in the same position relative to the transversal and a parallel line are **corresponding angles**. The diagram below has four pairs of corresponding angles: angles 1 and 5, angles 2 and 6, angles 3 and 7, and angles 4 and 8. Corresponding angles formed by parallel lines are congruent.

When two parallel lines are cut by a transversal, the two interior angles that are on opposite sides of the transversal are called **alternate interior angles**. In the diagram below, there are two pairs of alternate interior angles: angles 3 and 6, and angles 4 and 5. Alternate interior angles formed by parallel lines are congruent.

When two parallel lines are cut by a transversal, the two exterior angles that are on opposite sides of the transversal are called **alternate exterior angles**.

Review Video: Angles
Visit mometrix.com/academy and enter code: 264624

8

In the diagram below, there are two pairs of alternate exterior angles: angles 1 and 8, and angles 2 and 7. Alternate exterior angles formed by parallel lines are congruent.

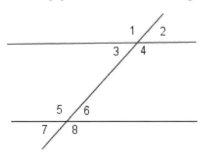

When two lines intersect, four angles are formed. The non-adjacent angles at this vertex are called vertical angles. Vertical angles are congruent. In the diagram, $\angle ABD \cong \angle CBE$ and $\angle ABC \cong \angle DBE$.

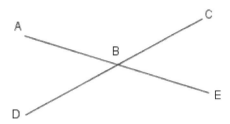

PRACTICE

P1. Find the measure of angles **(a)**, **(b)**, and **(c)** based on the figure with two parallel lines, two perpendicular lines and one transversal:

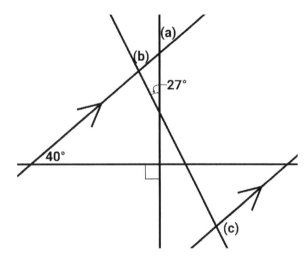

PRACTICE SOLUTIONS

P1. (a) The vertical angle paired with (a) is part of a right triangle with the 40° angle. Thus the measure can be found:

$$90° = 40° + a$$
$$a = 50°$$

9

(b) The triangle formed by the supplementary angle to (b) is part of a triangle with the vertical angle paired with (a) and the given angle of 27°. Since $a = 50°$:

$$180° = (180° - b) + 50° + 27°$$
$$103° = 180° - b$$
$$-77° = -b$$
$$77° = b$$

(c) As they are part of a transversal crossing parallel lines, angles (b) and (c) are supplementary. Thus $c = 103°$

$$V = \frac{1}{3}\pi r^2 h = \frac{1}{3}\pi(5 \text{ yd})^2(7 \text{ yd}) = \frac{35\pi}{3} \text{ yd}^3 \cong 36.65 \text{ yd}^3$$

Transformations

ROTATION

A **rotation** is a transformation that turns a figure around a point called the **center of rotation**, which can lie anywhere in the plane. If a line is drawn from a point on a figure to the center of rotation, and another line is drawn from the center to the rotated image of that point, the angle between the two lines is the **angle of rotation**. The vertex of the angle of rotation is the center of rotation.

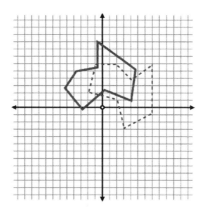

TRANSLATION AND DILATION

A **translation** is a transformation which slides a figure from one position in the plane to another position in the plane. The original figure and the translated figure have the same size, shape, and orientation. A **dilation** is a transformation which proportionally stretches or shrinks a figure by a

scale factor. The dilated image is the same shape and orientation as the original image but a different size. A polygon and its dilated image are similar.

Translation

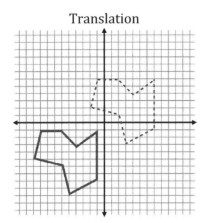

Dilation

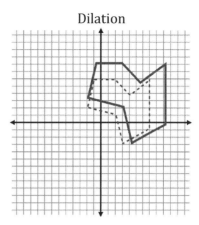

REFLECTION

A **reflection of a figure over a line** (a "flip") creates a congruent image that is the same distance from the line as the original figure but on the opposite side. The **line of reflection** is the perpendicular bisector of any line segment drawn from a point on the original figure to its reflected image (unless the point and its reflected image happen to be the same point, which happens when a figure is reflected over one of its own sides). A **reflection of a figure over a point** (an inversion) in two dimensions is the same as the rotation of the figure 180° about that point. The image of the figure is congruent to the original figure. The **point of reflection** is the midpoint of a line segment which connects a point in the figure to its image (unless the point and its reflected image happen to be the same point, which happens when a figure is reflected in one of its own points).

Reflection of a figure over a line

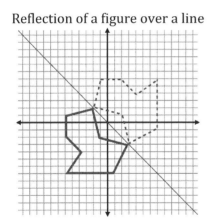

Reflection of a figure over a point

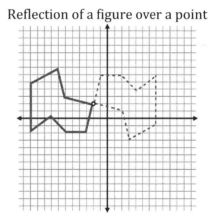

Review Video: Rotation
Visit mometrix.com/academy and enter code: 602600
Review Video: Translation
Visit mometrix.com/academy and enter code: 718628
Review Video: Dilation
Visit mometrix.com/academy and enter code: 471630
Review Video: Reflection
Visit mometrix.com/academy and enter code: 955068

PRACTICE

P1. Use the coordinate plane to reflect the figure below across the *y*-axis.

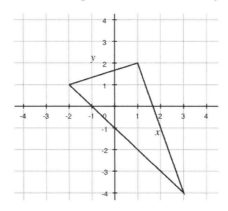

P2. Use the coordinate plane to enlarge the figure below by a factor of 2.

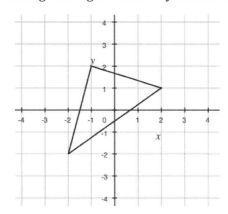

PRACTICE SOLUTIONS

P1. To reflect the image across the *y*-axis, replace each *x*-coordinate of the points that are the vertex of the triangle, *x*, with its negative, −*x*.

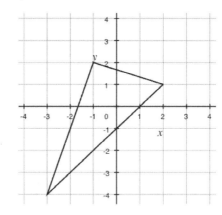

12

P2. An enlargement can be found by multiplying each coordinate of the coordinate pairs located at the triangle's vertices by 2. The original coordinates were $(-1, 2), (2, 1), (-2, -2)$, so the new coordinates are $(-2, 4), (4, 2), (-4, -4)$:

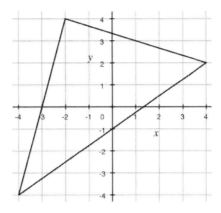

Two-Dimensional Shapes

POLYGONS

A **polygon** is a closed, two-dimensional figure with three or more straight line segments called **sides**. The point at which two sides of a polygon intersect is called the **vertex**. In a polygon, the number of sides is always equal to the number of vertices. A polygon with all sides congruent and all angles equal is called a **regular polygon**. Common polygons are:

$$\text{Triangle} = 3 \text{ sides}$$
$$\text{Quadrilateral} = 4 \text{ sides}$$
$$\text{Pentagon} = 5 \text{ sides}$$
$$\text{Hexagon} = 6 \text{ sides}$$
$$\text{Heptagon} = 7 \text{ sides}$$
$$\text{Octagon} = 8 \text{ sides}$$
$$\text{Nonagon} = 9 \text{ sides}$$
$$\text{Decagon} = 10 \text{ sides}$$
$$\text{Dodecagon} = 12 \text{ sides}$$

More generally, an n-gon is a polygon that has n angles and n sides.

The sum of the interior angles of an n-sided polygon is $(n - 2) \times 180°$. For example, in a triangle $n = 3$. So the sum of the interior angles is $(3 - 2) \times 180° = 180°$. In a quadrilateral, $n = 4$, and the sum of the angles is $(4 - 2) \times 180° = 360°$.

APOTHEM AND RADIUS

A line segment from the center of a polygon that is perpendicular to a side of the polygon is called the **apothem**. A line segment from the center of a polygon to a vertex of the polygon is called a

radius. In a regular polygon, the apothem can be used to find the area of the polygon using the formula $A = \frac{1}{2}ap$, where a is the apothem, and p is the perimeter.

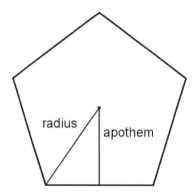

A **diagonal** is a line segment that joins two non-adjacent vertices of a polygon. The number of diagonals a polygon has can be found by using the formula:

$$\text{number of diagonals} = \frac{n(n-3)}{2}$$

Note that n is the number of sides in the polygon. This formula works for all polygons, not just regular polygons.

> **Review Video: Diagonals of Parallelograms, Rectangles, and Rhombi**
> Visit mometrix.com/academy and enter code: 320040

CONVEX AND CONCAVE POLYGONS

A **convex polygon** is a polygon whose diagonals all lie within the interior of the polygon. A **concave polygon** is a polygon with a least one diagonal that is outside the polygon. In the diagram below, quadrilateral *ABCD* is concave because diagonal $\overline{AC}$ lies outside the polygon and quadrilateral *EFGH* is convex because both diagonals lie inside the polygon

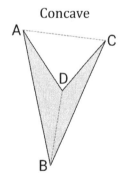
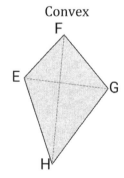

CONGRUENCE AND SIMILARITY

Congruent figures are geometric figures that have the same size and shape. All corresponding angles are equal, and all corresponding sides are equal. Congruence is indicated by the symbol ≅.

Congruent polygons

Similar figures are geometric figures that have the same shape, but do not necessarily have the same size. All corresponding angles are equal, and all corresponding sides are proportional, but they do not have to be equal. It is indicated by the symbol ~.

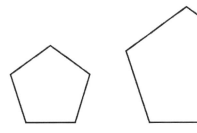

Similar polygons

Note that all congruent figures are also similar, but not all similar figures are congruent.

> **Review Video: Polygons, Similarity, and Congruence**
> Visit mometrix.com/academy and enter code: 686174
>
> **Review Video: Polygons**
> Visit mometrix.com/academy and enter code: 271869

LINE OF SYMMETRY

A line that divides a figure or object into congruent parts is called a **line of symmetry**. An object may have no lines of symmetry, one line of symmetry, or multiple (i.e., more than one) lines of symmetry.

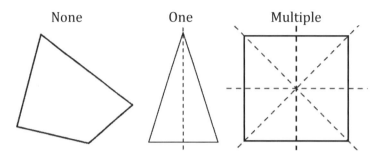

None   One   Multiple

> **Review Video: Symmetry**
> Visit mometrix.com/academy and enter code: 528106

TRIANGLES

A triangle is a three-sided figure with the sum of its interior angles being $180°$ The **perimeter of any triangle** is found by summing the three side lengths; $P = a + b + c$. For an equilateral triangle, this is the same as $P = 3a$, where a is any side length, since all three sides are the same length.

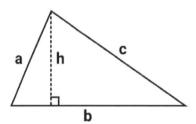

The **area of any triangle** can be found by taking half the product of one side length referred to as the base, often given the variable b and the perpendicular distance from that side to the opposite vertex called the altitude or height and given the variable h. In equation form that is $A = \frac{1}{2}bh$.

Another formula that works for any triangle is $A = \sqrt{s(s-a)(s-b)(s-c)}$, where s is the semiperimeter: $\frac{a+b+c}{2}$, and a, b, and c are the lengths of the three sides. Special cases include isosceles triangles: $A = \frac{1}{2}b\sqrt{a^2 - \frac{b^2}{4}}$, where b is the unique side and a is the length of one of the two congruent sides, and equilateral triangles: $A = \frac{\sqrt{3}}{4}a^2$, where a is the length of a side.

> **Review Video: Area and Perimeter of a Triangle**
> Visit mometrix.com/academy and enter code: 853779

PARTS OF A TRIANGLE

An **altitude** of a triangle is a line segment drawn from one vertex perpendicular to the opposite side. In the diagram below, $\overline{BE}$, $\overline{AD}$, and $\overline{CF}$ are altitudes. The length of an altitude is also called the height of the triangle. The three altitudes in a triangle are always concurrent. The point of concurrency of the altitudes of a triangle, O, is called the **orthocenter**. Note that in an obtuse triangle, the orthocenter will be outside the triangle, and in a right triangle, the orthocenter is the vertex of the right angle.

A **median** of a triangle is a line segment drawn from one vertex to the midpoint of the opposite side. In the diagram below, $\overline{BH}$, $\overline{AG}$, and $\overline{CI}$ are medians. This is not the same as the altitude, except the altitude to the base of an isosceles triangle and all three altitudes of an equilateral triangle. The point of concurrency of the medians of a triangle, T, is called the **centroid**. This is the same point as the orthocenter only in an equilateral triangle. Unlike the orthocenter, the centroid is always inside the triangle. The centroid can also be considered the exact center of the triangle. Any shape triangle can be perfectly balanced on a tip placed at the centroid. The centroid is also the point that is two-thirds the distance from the vertex to the opposite side.

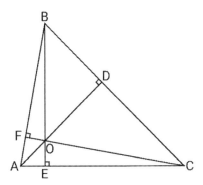
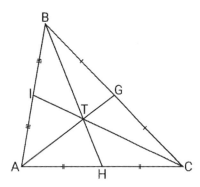

QUADRILATERALS

A **quadrilateral** is a closed two-dimensional geometric figure that has four straight sides. The sum of the interior angles of any quadrilateral is 360°.

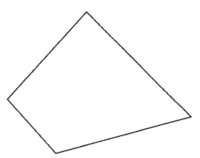

KITE

A **kite** is a quadrilateral with two pairs of adjacent sides that are congruent. A result of this is perpendicular diagonals. A kite can be concave or convex and has one line of symmetry.

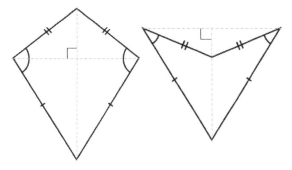

TRAPEZOID

Trapezoid: A trapezoid is defined as a quadrilateral that has at least one pair of parallel sides. There are no rules for the second pair of sides. So there are no rules for the diagonals and no lines of symmetry for a trapezoid.

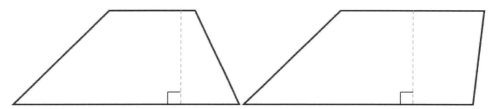

The **area of a trapezoid** is found by the formula $A = \frac{1}{2}h(b_1 + b_2)$, where h is the height (segment joining and perpendicular to the parallel bases), and b_1 and b_2 are the two parallel sides (bases). Do not use one of the other two sides as the height unless that side is also perpendicular to the parallel bases.

The **perimeter of a trapezoid** is found by the formula $P = a + b_1 + c + b_2$, where a, b_1, c, and b_2 are the four sides of the trapezoid.

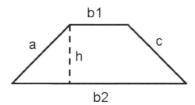

Review Video: Area and Perimeter of a Trapezoid
Visit mometrix.com/academy and enter code: 587523

Isosceles trapezoid: A trapezoid with equal base angles. This gives rise to other properties including: the two nonparallel sides have the same length, the two non-base angles are also equal, and there is one line of symmetry through the midpoints of the parallel sides.

PARALLELOGRAM

Parallelogram: A quadrilateral that has two pairs of opposite parallel sides. As such it is a special type of trapezoid. The sides that are parallel are also congruent. The opposite interior angles are always congruent, and the consecutive interior angles are supplementary. The diagonals of a parallelogram divide each other. Each diagonal divides the parallelogram into two congruent triangles. A parallelogram has no line of symmetry, but does have 180-degree rotational symmetry about the midpoint.

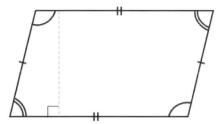

The **area of a parallelogram** is found by the formula $A = bh$, where b is the length of the base, and h is the height. Note that the base and height correspond to the length and width in a rectangle, so this formula would apply to rectangles as well. Do not confuse the height of a parallelogram with the length of the second side. The two are only the same measure in the case of a rectangle.

The **perimeter of a parallelogram** is found by the formula $P = 2a + 2b$ or $P = 2(a + b)$, where a and b are the lengths of the two sides.

> **Review Video: Parallelogram**
> Visit mometrix.com/academy and enter code: 129981
>
> **Review Video: Area and Perimeter of a Parallelogram**
> Visit mometrix.com/academy and enter code: 718313

RECTANGLE

Rectangle: A quadrilateral with four right angles. All rectangles are parallelograms and trapezoids, but not all parallelograms or trapezoids are rectangles. The diagonals of a rectangle are congruent. Rectangles have 2 lines of symmetry (through each pair of opposing midpoints) and 180-degree rotational symmetry about the midpoint.

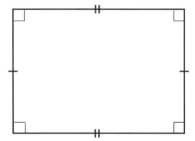

The **area of a rectangle** is found by the formula $A = lw$, where A is the area of the rectangle, l is the length (usually considered to be the longer side) and w is the width (usually considered to be the shorter side). The numbers for l and w are interchangeable.

The **perimeter of a rectangle** is found by the formula $P = 2l + 2w$ or $P = 2(l + w)$, where l is the length, and w is the width. It may be easier to add the length and width first and then double the result, as in the second formula.

> **Review Video: Area and Perimeter of a Rectangle**
> Visit mometrix.com/academy and enter code: 933707

RHOMBUS

Rhombus: A quadrilateral with four congruent sides. All rhombuses are parallelograms and kites; thus, they inherit all the properties of both types of quadrilaterals. The diagonals of a rhombus are perpendicular to each other. Rhombi have 2 lines of symmetry (along each of the diagonals) and 180-degree rotational symmetry. The **area of a rhombus** is half the product of the diagonals: $A = \frac{d_1 d_2}{2}$ and the perimeter of a rhombus is: $P = 2\sqrt{(d_1)^2 + (d_2)^2}$

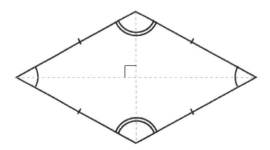

Review Video: <u>Area of a Trapezoid and Rhombus</u>
Visit mometrix.com/academy and enter code: 650047

SQUARE

Square: A quadrilateral with four right angles and four congruent sides. Squares satisfy the criteria of all other types of quadrilaterals. The diagonals of a square are congruent and perpendicular to each other. Squares have 4 lines of symmetry (through each pair of opposing midpoints and along each of the diagonals) as well as 90-degree rotational symmetry about the midpoint.

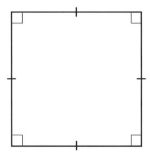

The **area of a square** is found by using the formula $A = s^2$, where s is the length of one side. The **perimeter of a square** is found by using the formula $P = 4s$, where s is the length of one side. Because all four sides are equal in a square, it is faster to multiply the length of one side by 4 than to add the same number four times. You could use the formulas for rectangles and get the same answer.

Review Video: <u>Area and Perimeter of a Square</u>
Visit mometrix.com/academy and enter code: 620902

HIERARCHY OF QUADRILATERALS

The hierarchy of quadrilaterals can be shown as follows:

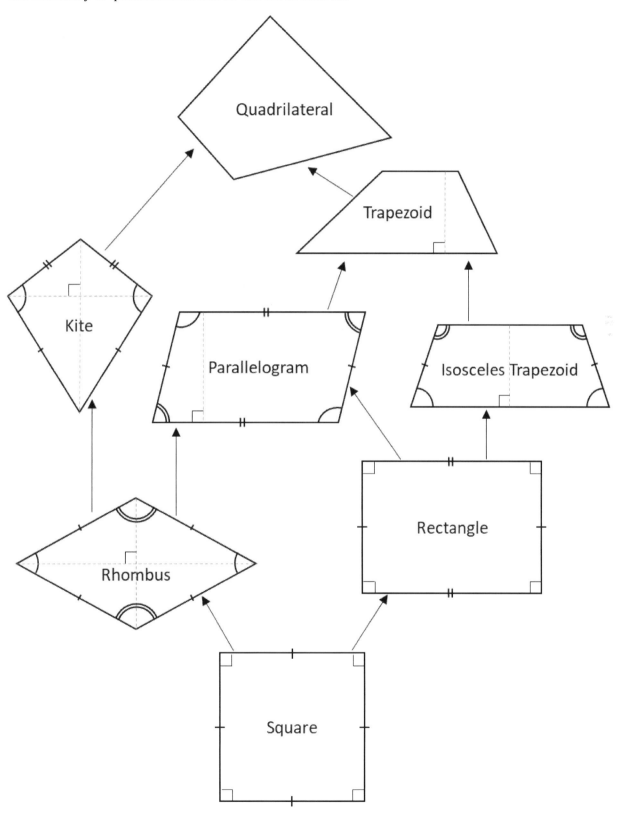

21

CIRCLES

The **center** of a circle is the single point from which every point on the circle is **equidistant**. The **radius** is a line segment that joins the center of the circle and any one point on the circle. All radii of a circle are equal. Circles that have the same center, but not the same length of radii are **concentric**. The **diameter** is a line segment that passes through the center of the circle and has both endpoints on the circle. The length of the diameter is exactly twice the length of the radius. Point O in the diagram below is the center of the circle, segments $\overline{OX}, \overline{OY}$, and $\overline{OZ}$ are radii, and segment $\overline{XZ}$ is a diameter.

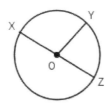

Review Video: <u>Points of a Circle</u>
Visit mometrix.com/academy and enter code: 420746

Review Video: <u>The Diameter, Radius, and Circumference of Circles</u>
Visit mometrix.com/academy and enter code: 448988

The **area of a circle** is found by the formula $A = \pi r^2$, where r is the length of the radius. If the diameter of the circle is given, remember to divide it in half to get the length of the radius before proceeding.

The **circumference** of a circle is found by the formula $C = 2\pi r$, where r is the radius. Again, remember to convert the diameter if you are given that measure rather than the radius.

Review Video: <u>Area and Circumference of a Circle</u>
Visit mometrix.com/academy and enter code: 243015

INSCRIBED AND CIRCUMSCRIBED FIGURES

These terms can both be used to describe a given arrangement of figures, depending on perspective. If each of the vertices of figure A lie on figure B, then it can be said that figure A is **inscribed** in figure B, but it can also be said that figure B is **circumscribed** about figure A. The following table and examples help to illustrate the concept. Note that the figures cannot both be circles, as they would be completely overlapping and neither would be inscribed or circumscribed.

Given	Description	Equivalent Description	Figures
Each of the sides of a pentagon is tangent to a circle	The circle is inscribed in the pentagon	The pentagon is circumscribed about the circle	
Each of the vertices of a pentagon lie on a circle	The pentagon is inscribed in the circle	The circle is circumscribed about the pentagon	

22

PRACTICE

P1. Find the area and perimeter of the following quadrilaterals:

  (a) A square with side length 2.5 cm.

  (b) A parallelogram with height 3 m, base 4 m, and other side 6 m.

  (c) A rhombus with diagonals 15 in and 20 in.

P2. Calculate the area of a triangle with side lengths of 7 ft, 8 ft, and 9 ft.

P3. Square ABCD is inscribed in a circle with radius 20 m. What is the area of the part of the circle outside of the square?

PRACTICE SOLUTIONS

P1. (a) $A = s^2 = (2.5 \text{ cm})^2 = 6.25 \text{ cm}^2$; $P = 4s = 4 \times 2.5 \text{ cm} = 10 \text{ cm}$

  (b) $A = bh = (3 \text{ m})(4 \text{ m}) = 12 \text{ m}^2$; $P = 2a + 2b = 2 \times 6 \text{ m} + 2 \times 4 \text{ m} = 20 \text{ m}$

  (c) $A = \frac{d_1 d_2}{2} = \frac{(15 \text{ in})(20 \text{ in})}{2} = 150 \text{ in}^2$;
  $P = 2\sqrt{(d_1)^2 + (d_2)^2} = 2\sqrt{(15 \text{ in})^2 + (20 \text{ in})^2} = 2\sqrt{625 \text{ in}^2} = 50 \text{ in}$

P2. Given only side lengths, we can use the semi perimeter to the find the area based on the formula, $A = \sqrt{s(s-a)(s-b)(s-c)}$, where s is the semiperimeter, $\frac{a+b+c}{2} = \frac{7+8+9}{2} = 12 \text{ ft}$:

$$A = \sqrt{12(12-7)(12-8)(12-9)}$$
$$= \sqrt{(12)(5)(4)(3)}$$
$$= 12\sqrt{5} \text{ ft}^2$$

P3. Begin by drawing a diagram of the situation, where we want to find the shaded area:

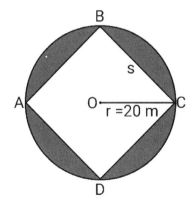
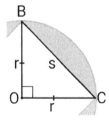

The area of the square is s^2, so the area we want to find is: $\pi r^2 - s^2$. Since the inscribed figure is a square, the triangle BCO is a 45-45-90 right triangle. Now we can find $s^2 = r^2 + r^2 = 2r^2$. So, the shaded area is:

$$A = \pi r^2 - s^2$$
$$= \pi r^2 - 2r^2$$
$$= (\pi - 2)r^2$$
$$= (\pi - 2) \times 400$$
$$\cong 456.6 \text{ m}^2$$

Three-Dimensional Shapes

SOLIDS

The **surface area of a solid object** is the area of all sides or exterior surfaces. For objects such as prisms and pyramids, a further distinction is made between base surface area (B) and lateral surface area (LA). For a prism, the total surface area (SA) is $SA = LA + 2B$. For a pyramid or cone, the total surface area is $SA = LA + B$.

> **Review Video: How to Calculate the Volume of 3D Objects**
> Visit mometrix.com/academy and enter code: 163343

The **surface area of a sphere** can be found by the formula $A = 4\pi r^2$, where r is the radius. The volume is given by the formula $V = \frac{4}{3}\pi r^3$, where r is the radius. Both quantities are generally given in terms of π.

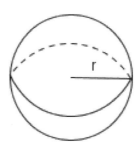

> **Review Video: Volume and Surface Area of a Sphere**
> Visit mometrix.com/academy and enter code: 786928

The **volume of any prism** is found by the formula $V = Bh$, where B is the area of the base, and h is the height (perpendicular distance between the bases). The surface area of any prism is the sum of the areas of both bases and all sides. It can be calculated as $SA = 2B + Ph$, where P is the perimeter of the base.

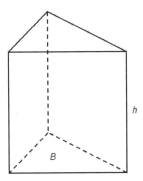

For a **rectangular prism**, the volume can be found by the formula $V = lwh$, where V is the volume, l is the length, w is the width, and h is the height. The surface area can be calculated as $SA = 2lw + 2hl + 2wh$ or $SA = 2(lw + hl + wh)$.

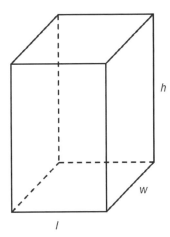

The **volume of a cube** can be found by the formula $V = s^3$, where s is the length of a side. The surface area of a cube is calculated as $SA = 6s^2$, where SA is the total surface area and s is the length of a side. These formulas are the same as the ones used for the volume and surface area of a rectangular prism, but simplified since all three quantities (length, width, and height) are the same.

> **Review Video: <u>Volume and Surface Area of a Cube</u>**
> Visit mometrix.com/academy and enter code: 664455

The **volume of a cylinder** can be calculated by the formula $V = \pi r^2 h$, where r is the radius, and h is the height. The surface area of a cylinder can be found by the formula $SA = 2\pi r^2 + 2\pi rh$. The first term is the base area multiplied by two, and the second term is the perimeter of the base multiplied by the height.

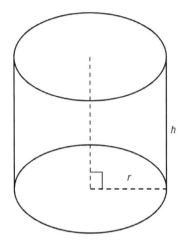

The **volume of a pyramid** is found by the formula $V = \frac{1}{3}Bh$, where B is the area of the base, and h is the height (perpendicular distance from the vertex to the base). Notice this formula is the same as $\frac{1}{3}$ times the volume of a prism. Like a prism, the base of a pyramid can be any shape.

Finding the **surface area of a pyramid** is not as simple as the other shapes we've looked at thus far. If the pyramid is a right pyramid, meaning the base is a regular polygon and the vertex is directly over the center of that polygon, the surface area can be calculated as $SA = B + \frac{1}{2}Ph_s$, where P is the perimeter of the base, and h_s is the slant height (distance from the vertex to the midpoint of one side of the base). If the pyramid is irregular, the area of each triangle side must be calculated individually and then summed, along with the base.

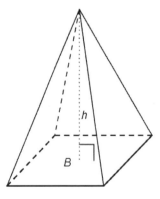

The **volume of a cone** is found by the formula $V = \frac{1}{3}\pi r^2 h$, where r is the radius, and h is the height. Notice this is the same as $\frac{1}{3}$ times the volume of a cylinder. The surface area can be calculated as $SA = \pi r^2 + \pi rs$, where s is the slant height. The slant height can be calculated using the Pythagorean theorem to be $\sqrt{r^2 + h^2}$, so the surface area formula can also be written as $SA = \pi r^2 + \pi r\sqrt{r^2 + h^2}$.

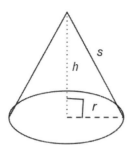

Review Video: Volume and Surface Area of a Right Circular Cone
Visit mometrix.com/academy and enter code: 573574

PRACTICE

P1. Find the surface area and volume of the following solids:

    (a) A cylinder with radius 5 m and height 0.5 m.

    (b) A trapezoidal prism with base area of 254 mm², base perimeter 74 mm, and height 10 mm.

    (c) A half sphere (radius 5 yds) on the base of an inverted cone with the same radius and a height of 7 yds.

PRACTICE SOLUTIONS

P1. (a) $SA = 2\pi r^2 + 2\pi rh = 2\pi(5 \text{ m})^2 + 2\pi(5 \text{ m})(0.5 \text{ m}) = 55\pi \text{ m}^2 \cong 172.79 \text{ m}^2$;
$V = \pi r^2 h = \pi(5 \text{ m})^2(0.5 \text{ m}) = 12.5\pi \text{ m}^3 \cong 39.27 \text{ m}^3$

(b) $SA = 2B + Ph = 2(254 \text{ mm}^2) + (74 \text{ mm})(10 \text{ mm}) = 1248 \text{ mm}^2$;
$V = Bh = (254 \text{ mm}^2)(10 \text{ mm}) = 2540 \text{ mm}^3$

(c) We can find s, the slant height using the Pythagorean theorem, and since this solid is made of parts of simple solids, we can combine the formulas to find surface area and volume:

$$s = \sqrt{r^2 + h^2} = \sqrt{(5 \text{ yd})^2 + (7 \text{ yd})^2} = \sqrt{74} \text{ yd}$$

$$SA_{Total} = (SA_{sphere})/2 + SA_{cone} - SA_{base}$$
$$= \frac{4\pi r^2}{2} + (\pi rs + \pi r^2) - \pi r^2$$
$$= 2\pi(5 \text{ yd})^2 + \pi(5 \text{ yd})(\sqrt{74} \text{ yd})$$
$$= 5\pi(10 + \sqrt{74}) \text{ yd}^2$$
$$\cong 292.20 \text{ yd}^2$$

$$V_{Total} = (V_{sphere})/2 + V_{cone}$$
$$= \frac{\frac{4}{3}\pi r^3}{2} + \frac{1}{3}\pi r^2 h$$
$$= \frac{2}{3}\pi(5 \text{ yd})^3 + \frac{1}{3}\pi(5 \text{ yd})^2(7 \text{ yd})$$
$$= \frac{5^2 \times \pi}{3}(10 + 7) \text{ yd}^3$$
$$\cong 445.06 \text{ yd}^3$$

Triangle Classification and Properties

CLASSIFICATIONS OF TRIANGLES

A **scalene triangle** is a triangle with no congruent sides. A scalene triangle will also have three angles of different measures. The angle with the largest measure is opposite the longest side, and the angle with the smallest measure is opposite the shortest side. An **acute triangle** is a triangle whose three angles are all less than 90°. If two of the angles are equal, the acute triangle is also an **isosceles triangle**. An isosceles triangle will also have two congruent angles opposite the two congruent sides. If the three angles are all equal, the acute triangle is also an **equilateral triangle**. An equilateral triangle will also have three congruent angles, each 60°. All equilateral triangles are also acute triangles. An **obtuse triangle** is a triangle with exactly one angle greater than 90°. The other two angles may or may not be equal. If the two remaining angles are equal, the obtuse triangle is also an isosceles triangle. A **right triangle** is a triangle with exactly one angle equal to 90°. All right triangles follow the Pythagorean theorem. A right triangle can never be acute or obtuse.

The table below illustrates how each descriptor places a different restriction on the triangle:

Angles ⟍ Sides	Acute: All angles < 90°	Obtuse: One angle > 90°	Right: One angle = 90°
Scalene: No equal side lengths	$90° > \angle a > \angle b > \angle c$ $x > y > z$	$\angle a > 90° > \angle b > \angle c$ $x > y > z$	$90° = \angle a > \angle b > \angle c$ $x > y > z$
Isosceles: Two equal side lengths	$90° > \angle a, \angle b,\, or\, \angle c$ $\angle b = \angle c,\quad y = z$	$\angle a > 90° > \angle b = \angle c$ $x > y = z$	$\angle a = 90°, \angle b = \angle c = 45°$ $x > y = z$
Equilateral: Three equal side lengths	$60° = \angle a = \angle b = \angle c$ $x = y = z$		

Review Video: Introduction to Types of Triangles
Visit mometrix.com/academy and enter code: 511711

SIMILARITY AND CONGRUENCE RULES

Similar triangles are triangles whose corresponding angles are equal and whose corresponding sides are proportional. Represented by AAA. Similar triangles whose corresponding sides are congruent are also congruent triangles.

Triangles can be shown to be **congruent** in 5 ways:

- **SSS**: Three sides of one triangle are congruent to the three corresponding sides of the second triangle.
- **SAS**: Two sides and the included angle (the angle formed by those two sides) of one triangle are congruent to the corresponding two sides and included angle of the second triangle.
- **ASA**: Two angles and the included side (the side that joins the two angles) of one triangle are congruent to the corresponding two angles and included side of the second triangle.
- **AAS**: Two angles and a non-included side of one triangle are congruent to the corresponding two angles and non-included side of the second triangle.
- **HL**: The hypotenuse and leg of one right triangle are congruent to the corresponding hypotenuse and leg of the second right triangle.

> **Review Video: Similar Triangles**
> Visit mometrix.com/academy and enter code: 398538

GENERAL RULES FOR TRIANGLES

The **triangle inequality theorem** states that the sum of the measures of any two sides of a triangle is always greater than the measure of the third side. If the sum of the measures of two sides were equal to the third side, a triangle would be impossible because the two sides would lie flat across the third side and there would be no vertex. If the sum of the measures of two of the sides was less than the third side, a closed figure would be impossible because the two shortest sides would never meet. In other words, for a triangle with sides lengths A, B, and C: $A + B > C$, $B + C > A$, and $A + C > B$

The sum of the measures of the interior angles of a triangle is always 180°. Therefore, a triangle can never have more than one angle greater than or equal to 90°.

In any triangle, the angles opposite congruent sides are congruent, and the sides opposite congruent angles are congruent. The largest angle is always opposite the longest side, and the smallest angle is always opposite the shortest side.

The line segment that joins the midpoints of any two sides of a triangle is always parallel to the third side and exactly half the length of the third side.

> **Review Video: General Rules (Triangle Inequality Theorem)**
> Visit mometrix.com/academy and enter code: 166488

PRACTICE

P1. Given the following pairs of triangles, determine whether they are similar, congruent, or neither (note that the figures are not drawn to scale):

(a).

(b).

(c).

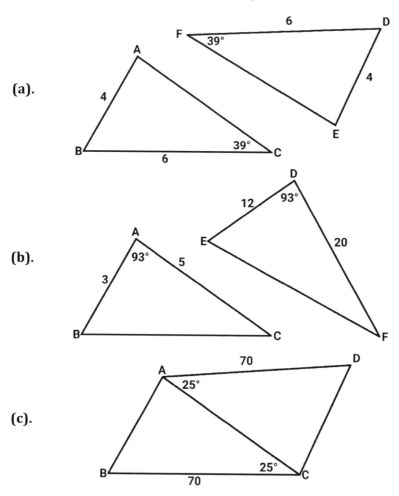

PRACTICE SOLUTIONS

P1. (a). Neither: We are given that two sides lengths and an angle are equal, however, the angle given is not between the given side lengths. That means there are two possible triangles that could satisfy the given measurements. Thus, we cannot be certain of congruence:

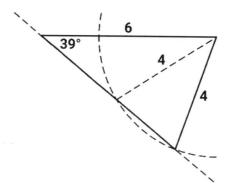

(b) Similar: Since we are given a side-angle-side of each triangle and the side lengths given are scaled evenly $\left(\frac{3}{5} \times \frac{4}{4} = \frac{12}{20}\right)$ and the angles are equal. Thus, $\Delta ABC \sim \Delta DEF$. If the side lengths were equal, then they would be congruent.

(c) Congruent: Even though we aren't given a measurement for the shared side of the figure, since it is shared it is equal. So, this is a case of SAS. Thus, $\Delta ABC \cong \Delta CDA$

Introductory Trigonometry

PYTHAGOREAN THEOREM

The side of a triangle opposite the right angle is called the **hypotenuse**. The other two sides are called the legs. The Pythagorean theorem states a relationship among the legs and hypotenuse of a right triangle: $a^2 + b^2 = c^2$, where a and b are the lengths of the legs of a right triangle, and c is the length of the hypotenuse. Note that this formula will only work with right triangles.

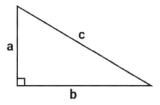

TRIGONOMETRIC FORMULAS

In the diagram below, angle C is the right angle, and side c is the hypotenuse. Side a is the side opposite to angle A and side b is the side opposite to angle B. Using ratios of side lengths as a means to calculate the sine, cosine, and tangent of an acute angle only works for right triangles.

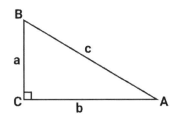

$$\sin A = \frac{\text{opposite side}}{\text{hypotenuse}} = \frac{a}{c} \qquad \csc A = \frac{1}{\sin A} = \frac{\text{hypotenuse}}{\text{opposite side}} = \frac{c}{a}$$

$$\cos A = \frac{\text{adjacent side}}{\text{hypotenuse}} = \frac{b}{c} \qquad \sec A = \frac{1}{\cos A} = \frac{\text{hypotenuse}}{\text{adjacent side}} = \frac{c}{b}$$

$$\tan A = \frac{\text{opposite side}}{\text{adjacent side}} = \frac{a}{b} \qquad \cot A = \frac{1}{\tan A} = \frac{\text{adjacent side}}{\text{opposite side}} = \frac{b}{a}$$

LAWS OF SINES AND COSINES

The **law of sines** states that $\frac{\sin A}{a} = \frac{\sin B}{b} = \frac{\sin C}{c}$, where A, B, and C are the angles of a triangle, and a, b, and c are the sides opposite their respective angles. This formula will work with all triangles, not just right triangles.

The **law of cosines** is given by the formula $c^2 = a^2 + b^2 - 2ab(\cos C)$, where a, b, and c are the sides of a triangle, and C is the angle opposite side c. This is a generalized form of the Pythagorean theorem that can be used on any triangle.

> **Review Video: Upper Level Trig (Law of Sines)**
> Visit mometrix.com/academy and enter code: 206844
>
> **Review Video: Law of Cosines**
> Visit mometrix.com/academy and enter code: 158911

PRACTICE

P1. Calculate the following values based on triangle MNO:

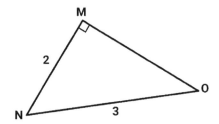

(a) length of $\overline{MO}$

(b) $\sin(\angle NOM)$

(c) area of the triangle, if the units of the measurements are in miles

PRACTICE SOLUTIONS

P1. (a) Since triangle MNO is a right triangle, we can use the simple form of Pythagoras theorem to find the missing side length:

$$\left(\overline{MO}\right)^2 + 2^2 = 3^2$$
$$\left(\overline{MO}\right)^2 = 9 - 4$$
$$\overline{MO} = \sqrt{5}$$

(b) Recall that sine of an angle in a right triangle is the ratio of the opposite side to the hypotenuse. So, $\sin(\angle NOM) = 2/3$

(c) Since triangle MNO is a right triangle, we can use either of the legs as the height and the other as the base in the simple formula for the area of a triangle:

$$A = \frac{bh}{2}$$
$$= \frac{(2 \text{ mi})\left(\sqrt{5} \text{ mi}\right)}{2}$$
$$= \sqrt{5} \text{ mi}^2$$

Circle Properties

ARCS

An **arc** is a portion of a circle. Specifically, an arc is the set of points between and including two points on a circle. An arc does not contain any points inside the circle. When a segment is drawn from the endpoints of an arc to the center of the circle, a sector is formed. A **minor arc** is an arc that has a measure less than 180°. A **major arc** is an arc that has a measure of at least 180°. Every minor arc has a corresponding major arc that can be found by subtracting the measure of the minor arc from 360°. A **semicircle** is an arc whose endpoints are the endpoints of the diameter of a circle. A semicircle is exactly half of a circle.

Arc length is the length of that portion of the circumference between two points on the circle. The formula for arc length is $s = \frac{\pi r \theta}{180°}$ where s is the arc length, r is the length of the radius, and θ is the angular measure of the arc in degrees, or $s = r\theta$, where θ is the angular measure of the arc in radians (2π radians = 360 degrees).

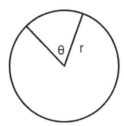

ANGLES OF CIRCLES

A **central angle** is an angle whose vertex is the center of a circle and whose legs intercept an arc of the circle. The measure of a central angle is equal to the measure of the minor arc it intercepts.

An **inscribed angle** is an angle whose vertex lies on a circle and whose legs contain chords of that circle. The portion of the circle intercepted by the legs of the angle is called the intercepted arc. The measure of the intercepted arc is exactly twice the measure of the inscribed angle. In the following diagram, angle ABC is an inscribed angle. $\widehat{AC} = 2(\text{m}\angle ABC)$

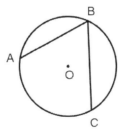

Any angle inscribed in a semicircle is a right angle. The intercepted arc is 180°, making the inscribed angle half that, or 90°. In the diagram below, angle ABC is inscribed in semicircle ABC, making angle ABC equal to 90°.

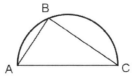

33

SECANTS, CHORDS, AND TANGENTS

A **secant** is a line that intersects a circle in two points. The segment of a secant line that is contained within the circle is called a **chord**. Two secants may intersect inside the circle, on the circle, or outside the circle. When the two secants intersect on the circle, an inscribed angle is formed. When two secants intersect inside a circle, the measure of each of two vertical angles is equal to half the sum of the two intercepted arcs. Consider the following diagram where $m\angle AEB = \frac{1}{2}(\widehat{AB} + \widehat{CD})$ and $m\angle BEC = \frac{1}{2}(\widehat{BC} + \widehat{AD})$.

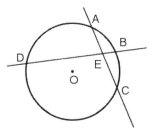

When two secants intersect outside a circle, the measure of the angle formed is equal to half the difference of the two arcs that lie between the two secants. In the diagram below, $m\angle AEB = \frac{1}{2}(\widehat{AB} - \widehat{CD})$.

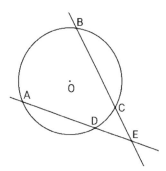

A **tangent** is a line in the same plane as a circle that touches the circle in exactly one point. The point at which a tangent touches a circle is called the **point of tangency**. While a line segment can be tangent to a circle as part of a line that is tangent, it is improper to say a tangent can be simply a line segment that touches the circle in exactly one point.

In the diagram below, $\overleftrightarrow{EB}$ is a secant and contains chord $\overline{EB}$ and $\overleftrightarrow{CD}$ is tangent to circle A. Notice that $\overline{FB}$ is not tangent to the circle. $\overline{FB}$ is a line segment that touches the circle in exactly one point, but if the segment were extended, it would touch the circle in a second point. In the diagram below, point B is the point of tangency.

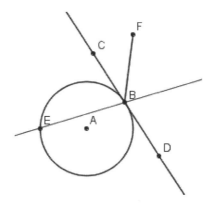

SECTORS

A **sector** is the portion of a circle formed by two radii and their intercepted arc. While the arc length is exclusively the points that are also on the circumference of the circle, the sector is the entire area bounded by the arc and the two radii.

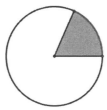

The **area of a sector** of a circle is found by the formula, $A = \frac{\theta r^2}{2}$, where A is the area, θ is the measure of the central angle in radians, and r is the radius. To find the area with the central angle in degrees, use the formula, $A = \frac{\theta \pi r^2}{360}$, where θ is the measure of the central angle and r is the radius.

PRACTICE

P1. Given that $\angle DEB = 80°$ and $\widehat{BC} = 90°$, determine the following values based on the figure:

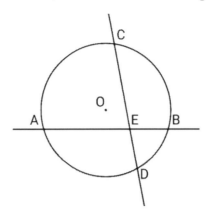

    (a) $\widehat{AD}$

    (b) $\widehat{DB} + \widehat{CA}$

P2. Given that $\angle OCB = 50°$, $\overleftrightarrow{EF}$ is tangent to the circle at B, and $\overline{CB} = 6$ km, determine the following values based on the figure:

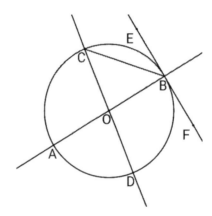

    (a) The angle made between $\overleftrightarrow{CD}$ and a line tangent to the circle at A.

    (b) The area of the sector of the circle between C and B.

PRACTICE SOLUTIONS

P1. (a). Recall that when two secants intersect inside of a circle, the measure of each of two vertical angles is equal to half the sum of the two intercepted arcs. Also, since $\angle DEB$ and $\angle CEB$ are supplementary, the measure of $\angle CEB = 180° - 80° = 100°$. In other words:

$$\angle CEB = \frac{1}{2}\left(\widehat{BC} + \widehat{AD}\right)$$
$$100° = \frac{1}{2}\left(90° + \widehat{AD}\right)$$
$$200° = 90° + \widehat{AD}$$
$$110° = \widehat{AD}$$

(b) Note that the whole circle is divided into four arcs. Thus,

$$\widehat{AD} + \widehat{DB} + \widehat{BC} + \widehat{CA} = 360°$$
$$110° + \widehat{DB} + 90° + \widehat{CA} = 360°$$
$$\widehat{DB} + \widehat{CA} = 160°$$

P2. (a) A line tangent to the circle at A creates a right triangle with one vertex at O, one at A, and the final vertex where $\overleftrightarrow{CD}$ intersects the tangent line, let us call that point G.

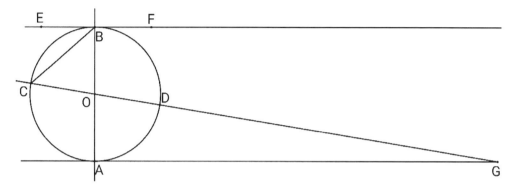

Since AB is a diameter, the line tangent at A is perpendicular to AB, so $\angle OAG = 90°$. The triangle COB has two legs that are the radius of the circle and so must be isosceles. So, $50° × 2 + \angle COB = 180°$, which means that $\angle COB$ and the vertical angle $\angle GOA$ both equal 80°. Knowing this we can find $\angle AGO$:

$$80° + 90° + \angle AGO = 180°$$
$$\angle AGO = 10°$$

(b) We know $\angle OCB = 50°$ and that triangle COB is isosceles with two legs equal to the radius, so a perpendicular bisector of the triangle as shown will create a right triangle:

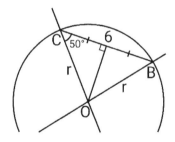 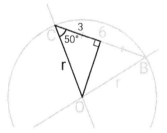

Recall that the cosine of an angle in a right triangle is the ratio of the adjacent side to the hypotenuse. Thus, we can find r:

$$\cos 50° = \frac{3}{r}$$
$$r = \frac{3}{\cos 50°}$$

As noted in part (a), $\angle COB = 80°$, so the area of the sector is:

$$A = \frac{\theta \pi r^2}{360°}$$

$$= \frac{80° \pi \left(\frac{3}{\cos 50°}\right)^2}{360°}$$

$$= \frac{2\pi \left(\frac{9}{\cos^2 50°}\right)}{9}$$

$$= \frac{2\pi}{\cos^2 50°} \cong 15.2 \text{ km}^2$$

Conic Sections

CONIC SECTIONS

Conic sections are a family of shapes that can be thought of as cross sections of a pair of infinite right cones stacked vertex to vertex. This is easiest to see with a visual representation:

A three-dimensional look at representative conic sections. (Note that a hyperbola intersects both cones.)

A side-on look at representative conic sections. (Note that the parabola is parallel to the slant of the cones.)

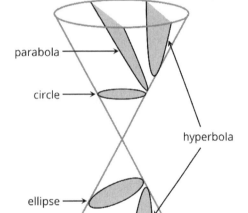

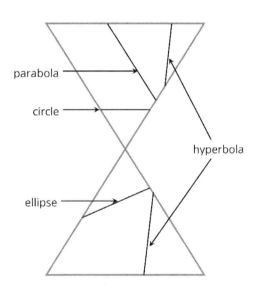

In short, a circle is a horizontal cross section, a parabola is a cross section parallel to the slant of the cone, an ellipse is a cross section at an angle *less than* the slant of the cone, and a hyperbola is a cross section at an angle *greater than* the slant of the cone.

ELLIPSE

An **ellipse** is the set of all points in a plane whose total distance from two fixed points called the **foci** (singular: focus) is constant, and whose center is the midpoint between the foci.

The standard equation of an ellipse that is taller than it is wide is $\frac{(x-h)^2}{a^2} + \frac{(y-k)^2}{b^2} = 1$, where a and b are coefficients. The center is the point (h, k) and the foci are the points $(h, k + c)$ and $(h, k - c)$, where $c^2 = a^2 - b^2$ and $a^2 > b^2$.

The major axis has length $2a$, and the minor axis has length $2b$.

Eccentricity (e) is a measure of how elongated an ellipse is, and is the ratio of the distance between the foci to the length of the major axis. Eccentricity will have a value between 0 and 1. The closer to 1 the eccentricity is, the closer the ellipse is to being a circle. The formula for eccentricity is $= \frac{c}{a}$.

PARABOLA

A **parabola** is the set of all points in a plane that are equidistant from a fixed line, called the **directrix**, and a fixed point not on the line, called the **focus**. The **axis** is the line perpendicular to the directrix that passes through the focus.

For parabolas that open up or down, the standard equation is $(x - h)^2 = 4c(y - k)$, where h, c, and k are coefficients. If c is positive, the parabola opens up. If c is negative, the parabola opens down. The vertex is the point (h, k). The directrix is the line having the equation $y = -c + k$, and the focus is the point $(h, c + k)$.

For parabolas that open left or right, the standard equation is $(y - k)^2 = 4c(x - h)$, where k, c, and h are coefficients. If c is positive, the parabola opens to the right. If c is negative, the parabola opens to the left. The vertex is the point (h, k). The directrix is the line having the equation $x = -c + h$, and the focus is the point $(c + h, k)$.

> **Review Video: Parabolas**
> Visit mometrix.com/academy and enter code: 129187

HYPERBOLA

A **hyperbola** is the set of all points in a plane, whose distance from two fixed points, called foci, has a constant difference.

The standard equation of a horizontal hyperbola is $\frac{(x-h)^2}{a^2} - \frac{(y-k)^2}{b^2} = 1$, where a, b, h, and k are real numbers. The center is the point (h, k), the vertices are the points $(h + a, k)$ and $(h - a, k)$, and the foci are the points that every point on one of the parabolic curves is equidistant from. The foci are found using the formulas $(h + c, k)$ and $(h - c, k)$, where $c^2 = a^2 + b^2$. The asymptotes are two lines the graph of the hyperbola approaches but never reaches, and are given by the equations $y = \left(\frac{b}{a}\right)(x - h) + k$ and $y = -\left(\frac{b}{a}\right)(x - h) + k$.

The standard equation of a vertical hyperbola is $\frac{(y-k)^2}{a^2} - \frac{(x-h)^2}{b^2} = 1$, where a, b, k, and h are real numbers. The center is the point (h, k), the vertices are the points $(h, k + a)$ and $(h, k - a)$, and the foci are the points that every point on one of the hyperbolic curves is equidistant from and are found using the formulas $(h, k + c)$ and $(h, k - c)$, where $c^2 = a^2 + b^2$. The asymptotes are two lines the graph of the hyperbola approaches but never reaches, and are given by the equations $y = \left(\frac{a}{b}\right)(x - h) + k$ and $y = -\left(\frac{a}{b}\right)(x - h) + k$.

Trigonometry

DEGREES, RADIANS, AND THE UNIT CIRCLE

It is important to understand the deep connection between trigonometry and circles. Specifically, the two main units, **degrees** (°) and **radians** (rad), that are used to measure angles are related this way: 360° in one full circle and 2π radians in one full circle: $360° = 2\pi$ rad. The conversion factor relating the two is often stated as $\frac{180°}{\pi}$. For example, to convert $\frac{3\pi}{2}$ radians to degrees, multiply by the conversion factor: $\frac{3\pi}{2} \times \frac{180°}{\pi} = 270°$. As another example, to convert 60° to radians, divide by the conversion factor or multiply by the reciprocal: $60° \times \frac{\pi}{180°} = \frac{\pi}{3}$ radians.

Recall that the standard equation for a circle is $(x - h)^2 + (y - k)^2 = r^2$. A **unit circle** is a circle with a radius of 1 ($r = 1$) that has its center at the origin ($h = 0, k = 0$). Thus, the equation for the unit circle simplifies from the standard equation down to $x^2 + y^2 = 1$.

Standard position is the position of an angle of measure θ whose vertex is at the origin, the initial side crosses the unit circle at the point $(1, 0)$, and the terminal side crosses the unit circle at some other point (a, b). In the standard position, $\sin\theta = b$, $\cos\theta = a$, and $\tan\theta = \frac{b}{a}$.

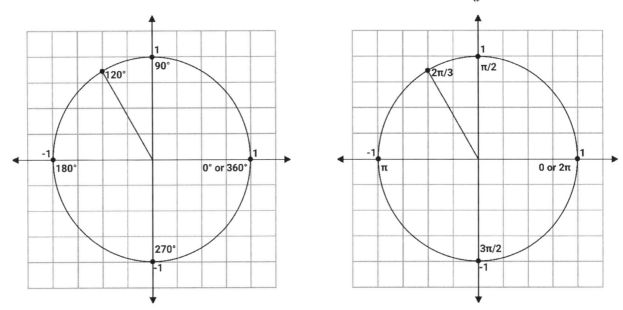

Review Video: Unit Circles and Standard Position
Visit mometrix.com/academy and enter code: 333922

BASIC TRIGONOMETRIC FUNCTIONS

SINE

The **sine** (sin) function has a period of 360° or 2π radians. This means that its graph makes one complete cycle every 360° or 2π. Because $\sin 0 = 0$, the graph of $y = \sin x$ begins at the origin, with the x-axis representing the angle measure, and the y-axis representing the sine of the angle. The graph of the sine function is a smooth curve that begins at the origin, peaks at the point $\left(\frac{\pi}{2}, 1\right)$, crosses the x-axis at $(\pi, 0)$, has its lowest point at $\left(\frac{3\pi}{2}, -1\right)$, and returns to the x-axis to complete one cycle at $(2\pi, 0)$.

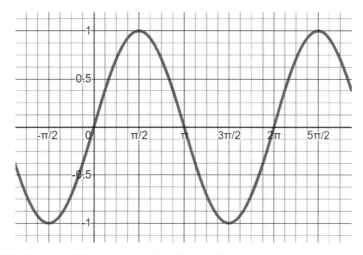

COSINE

The **cosine** (cos) function also has a period of 360° or 2π radians, which means that its graph also makes one complete cycle every 360° or 2π. Because $\cos 0° = 1$, the graph of $y = \cos x$ begins at the point $(0, 1)$, with the x-axis representing the angle measure, and the y-axis representing the cosine of the angle. The graph of the cosine function is a smooth curve that begins at the point $(0, 1)$, crosses the x-axis at the point $\left(\frac{\pi}{2}, 0\right)$, has its lowest point at $(\pi, -1)$, crosses the x-axis again at the point $\left(\frac{3\pi}{2}, 0\right)$, and returns to a peak at the point $(2\pi, 1)$ to complete one cycle.

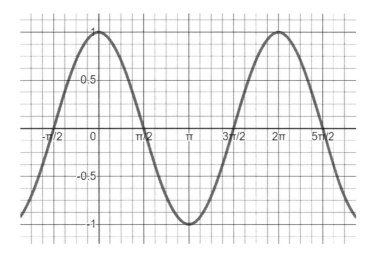

TANGENT

The **tangent** (tan) function has a period of 180° or π radians, which means that its graph makes one complete cycle every 180° or π radians. The x-axis represents the angle measure, and the y-axis represents the tangent of the angle. The graph of the tangent function is a series of smooth curves that cross the *x*-axis at every 180° or π radians and have an asymptote every $k \times 90°$ or $\frac{k\pi}{2}$ radians, where k is an odd integer. This can be explained by the fact that the tangent is calculated by dividing the sine by the cosine, since the cosine equals zero at those asymptote points.

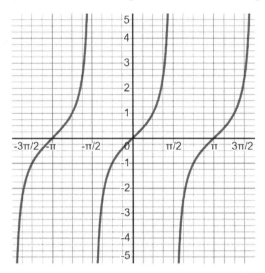

DEFINED AND RECIPROCAL FUNCTIONS

The tangent function is defined as the ratio of the sine to the cosine: $\tan x = \frac{\sin x}{\cos x}$

To take the reciprocal of a number means to place that number as the denominator of a fraction with a numerator of 1. The reciprocal functions are thus defined quite simply.

Cosecant	$\csc x$	$\dfrac{1}{\sin x}$
Secant	$\sec x$	$\dfrac{1}{\cos x}$
Cotangent	$\cot x$	$\dfrac{1}{\tan x}$

It is important to know these reciprocal functions, but they are not as commonly used as the three basic functions.

INVERSE FUNCTIONS

Each of the trigonometric functions accepts an angular measure, either degrees or radians, and gives a numerical value as the output. The inverse functions do the opposite; they accept a numerical value and give an angular measure as the output. The inverse of sine, or arcsine, commonly written as either $\sin^{-1} x$ or $\arcsin x$, gives the angle whose sine is x. Similarly:

The inverse of $\cos x$ is written as $\cos^{-1} x$ or $\arccos x$ and means the angle whose cosine is x.
The inverse of $\tan x$ is written as $\tan^{-1} x$ or $\arctan x$ and means the angle whose tangent is x.
The inverse of $\csc x$ is written as $\csc^{-1} x$ or $\text{arccsc } x$ and means the angle whose cosecant is x.
The inverse of $\sec x$ is written as $\sec^{-1} x$ or $\text{arcsec } x$ and means the angle whose secant is x.
The inverse of $\cot x$ is written as $\cot^{-1} x$ or $\text{arccot } x$ and means the angle whose cotangent is x.

> **Review Video: Inverse of a Cosine**
> Visit mometrix.com/academy and enter code: 156054
>
> **Review Video: Inverse of a Tangent**
> Visit mometrix.com/academy and enter code: 229055

IMPORTANT NOTE ABOUT SOLVING TRIGONOMETRIC EQUATIONS

Trigonometric and algebraic equations are solved following the same rules, but while algebraic expressions have one unique solution, trigonometric equations could have multiple solutions, and you must find them all. When solving for an angle with a known trigonometric value, you must consider the sign and include all angles with that value. Your calculator will probably only give one value as an answer, typically in the following ranges:

- For $\sin^{-1} x$, $\left[-\frac{\pi}{2}, \frac{\pi}{2}\right]$ or $[-90°, 90°]$
- For $\cos^{-1} x$, $[0, \pi]$ or $[0°, 180°]$
- For $\tan^{-1} x$, $\left[-\frac{\pi}{2}, \frac{\pi}{2}\right]$ or $[-90°, 90°]$

It is important to determine if there is another angle in a different quadrant that also satisfies the problem. To do this, find the other quadrant(s) with the same sign for that trigonometric function and find the angle that has the same reference angle. Then check whether this angle is also a solution.

- In the first quadrant, all six trigonometric functions are positive.
- In the second quadrant, sin and csc are positive.
- In the third quadrant, tan and cot are positive.
- In the fourth quadrant, cos and sec are positive.

If you remember the phrase, "ALL Students Take Classes," you will be able to remember the sign of each trigonometric function in each quadrant. ALL represents all the signs in the first quadrant. The "S" in "Students" represents the sine function and its reciprocal in the second quadrant. The "T" in "Take" represents the tangent function and its reciprocal in the third quadrant. The "C" in "Classes" represents the cosine function and its reciprocal.

DOMAIN, RANGE, AND ASYMPTOTES IN TRIGONOMETRY

The domain is the set of all possible real number values of x on the graph of a trigonometric function. Some graphs will impose limits on the values of x.

The range is the set of all possible real number values of y on the graph of a trigonometric function. Some graphs will impose limits on the values of y.

Asymptotes are lines which the graph of a trigonometric function approaches but never reaches. Asymptotes exist for values of x in the graphs of the tangent, cotangent, secant, and cosecant. The sine and cosine graphs do not have any asymptotes.

DOMAIN, RANGE, AND ASYMPTOTES OF THE SIX TRIGONOMETRIC FUNCTIONS

The domain, range, and asymptotes for each of the trigonometric functions are as follows:

- In the **sine** function, the domain is all real numbers, the range is $-1 \leq y \leq 1$, and there are no asymptotes.
- In the **cosine** function, the domain is all real numbers; the range is $-1 \leq y \leq 1$, and there are no asymptotes.
- In the **tangent** function, the domain is $x \in$ all real numbers; $x \neq \frac{\pi}{2} + k\pi$, the range is all real numbers; and the asymptotes are the lines $x = \frac{\pi}{2} + k\pi$.
- In the **cosecant** function, the domain is $x \in$ all real numbers; $x \neq k\pi$, the range is $(-\infty, -1]$ and $[1, \infty)$, and the asymptotes are the lines $x = k\pi$.
- In the **secant** function, the domain is $x \in$ all real numbers; $x \neq \frac{\pi}{2} + k\pi$, the range is $(-\infty, 1]$ and $[1, \infty)$, and the asymptotes are the lines $x = \frac{\pi}{2} + k\pi$.
- In the **cotangent** function, the domain is $x \in$ all real numbers; $x \neq k\pi$, the range is all real numbers, and the asymptotes are the lines $x = k\pi$.

In each of the above cases, k represents any integer.

TRIGONOMETRIC IDENTITIES
SUM AND DIFFERENCE

To find the sine, cosine, or tangent of the sum or difference of two angles, use one of the following formulas where α and β are two angles with known sine, cosine, or tangent values as needed:

$$\sin(\alpha \pm \beta) = \sin\alpha \cos\beta \pm \cos\alpha \sin\beta$$
$$\cos(\alpha \pm \beta) = \cos\alpha \cos\beta \mp \sin\alpha \sin\beta$$
$$\tan(\alpha \pm \beta) = \frac{\tan\alpha \pm \tan\beta}{1 \mp \tan\alpha \tan\beta}$$

HALF ANGLE

To find the sine or cosine of half of a known angle, use the following formulas where θ is an angle with a known exact cosine value:

$$\sin(\theta/2) = \pm\sqrt{(1 - cos\theta)/2}$$
$$\cos(\theta/2) = \pm\sqrt{(1 + \cos\theta)/2}$$

To determine the sign of the answer, you must recognize which quadrant the given angle is in and apply the correct sign for the trigonometric function you are using. If you need to find an expression for the exact sine or cosine of an angle that you do not know, such as sine 22.5°, you can rewrite the given angle as a half angle, such as $\sin\left(\frac{45°}{2}\right)$, and use the formula above:

$$\sin\left(\frac{45°}{2}\right) = \pm\sqrt{(1 - \cos(45°))/2} = \pm\sqrt{\left(1 - \frac{\sqrt{2}}{2}\right)/2} = \pm\sqrt{(2 - \sqrt{2})/4} = \pm\frac{1}{2}\sqrt{(2 - \sqrt{2})}$$

To find the tangent or cotangent of half of a known angle, use the following formulas where θ is an angle with known exact sine and cosine values:

$$\tan\frac{\theta}{2} = \frac{sin\theta}{1 + \cos\theta}$$
$$\cot\frac{\theta}{2} = \frac{\sin\theta}{1 - \cos\theta}$$

These formulas will work for finding the tangent or cotangent of half of any angle unless the cosine of θ happens to make the denominator of the identity equal to 0.

The Pythagorean theorem states that $a^2 + b^2 = c^2$ for all right triangles. The trigonometric identity that derives from this principle is stated in this way: $\sin^2\theta + \cos^2\theta = 1$

Dividing each term by either $\sin^2\theta$ or $\cos^2\theta$ yields two other identities, respectively:

$$1 + \cot^2\theta = \csc^2\theta$$
$$\tan^2\theta + 1 = \sec^2\theta$$

DOUBLE ANGLES

In each case, use one of the double angle formulas. To find the sine or cosine of twice a known angle, use one of the following formulas:

$$\sin(2\theta) = 2\sin\theta\cos\theta$$

$$\cos(2\theta) = \cos^2\theta - \sin^2\theta$$
$$= 2\cos^2\theta - 1$$
$$= 1 - 2\sin^2\theta$$

To find the tangent or cotangent of twice a known angle, use the formulas where θ is an angle with known exact sine, cosine, tangent, and cotangent values:

$$\tan(2\theta) = \frac{2\tan\theta}{1 - \tan^2\theta}$$
$$\cot(2\theta) = \frac{\cot\theta - \tan\theta}{2}$$

PRODUCTS

To find the product of the sines and cosines of two different angles, use one of the following formulas where α and β are two unique angles:

$$\sin\alpha\sin\beta = \frac{1}{2}[\cos(\alpha - \beta) - \cos(\alpha + \beta)]$$
$$\cos\alpha\cos\beta = \frac{1}{2}[\cos(\alpha + \beta) + \cos(\alpha - \beta)]$$
$$\sin\alpha\cos\beta = \frac{1}{2}[\sin(\alpha + \beta) + \sin(\alpha - \beta)]$$
$$\cos\alpha\sin\beta = \frac{1}{2}[\sin(\alpha + \beta) - \sin(\alpha - \beta)]$$

COMPLEMENTARY

The trigonometric cofunction identities use the trigonometric relationships of complementary angles (angles whose sum is 90°). These are:

$$\cos x = \sin(90° - x)$$
$$\csc x = \sec(90° - x)$$
$$\cot x = \tan(90° - x)$$

TABLE OF COMMONLY ENCOUNTERED ANGLES

$0° = 0$ radians, $30° = \frac{\pi}{6}$ radians, $45° = \frac{\pi}{4}$ radians, $60° = \frac{\pi}{3}$ radians, and $90° = \frac{\pi}{2}$ radians

$\sin 0° = 0$	$\cos 0° = 1$	$\tan 0° = 0$
$\sin 30° = \frac{1}{2}$	$\cos 30° = \frac{\sqrt{3}}{2}$	$\tan 30° = \frac{\sqrt{3}}{3}$
$\sin 45° = \frac{\sqrt{2}}{2}$	$\cos 45° = \frac{\sqrt{2}}{2}$	$\tan 45° = 1$
$\sin 60° = \frac{\sqrt{3}}{2}$	$\cos 60° = \frac{1}{2}$	$\tan 60° = \sqrt{3}$
$\sin 90° = 1$	$\cos 90° = 0$	$\tan 90° =$ undefined
$\csc 0° =$ undefined	$\sec 0° = 1$	$\cot 0° =$ undefined
$\csc 30° = 2$	$\sec 30° = \frac{2\sqrt{3}}{3}$	$\cot 30° = \sqrt{3}$
$\csc 45° = \sqrt{2}$	$\sec 45° = \sqrt{2}$	$\cot 45° = 1$
$\csc 60° = \frac{2\sqrt{3}}{3}$	$\sec 60° = 2$	$\cot 60° = \frac{\sqrt{3}}{3}$
$\csc 90° = 1$	$\sec 90° =$ undefined	$\cot 90° = 0$

The values in the upper half of this table are values you should have memorized or be able to find quickly and those in the lower half can easily be determined as the reciprocal of the corresponding function.

RECTANGULAR AND POLAR COORDINATES

Rectangular coordinates are those that lie on the square grids of the Cartesian plane. They should be quite familiar to you. The polar coordinate system is based on a circular graph, rather than the square grid of the Cartesian system. Points in the polar coordinate system are in the format (r, θ), where r is the distance from the origin (think radius of the circle) and θ is the smallest positive angle (moving counterclockwise around the circle) made with the positive horizontal axis.

To convert a point from rectangular (x, y) format to polar (r, θ) format, use the formula (x, y) to $(r, \theta) \Rightarrow r = \sqrt{x^2 + y^2}; \theta = \arctan\frac{y}{x}$ when $x \neq 0$

If x is positive, use the positive square root value for r. If x is negative, use the negative square root value for r. If $x = 0$, use the following rules:

- If $y = 0$, then $\theta = 0$
- If $y > 0$, then $\theta = \frac{\pi}{2}$
- If $y < 0$, then $\theta = \frac{3\pi}{2}$

To convert a point from polar (r, θ) format to rectangular (x, y) format, use the formula (r, θ) to $(x, y) \Rightarrow x = r \cos\theta ; y = r \sin\theta$

DE MOIVRE'S THEOREM

De Moivre's theorem is used to find the powers of complex numbers (numbers that contain the imaginary number i) written in polar form. Given a trigonometric expression that contains i, such as $z = r \cos x + ir \sin x$, where r is a real number and x is an angle measurement in polar form, use the formula $z^n = r^n(\cos nx + i \sin nx)$, where r and n are real numbers, x is the angle measure in polar form, and i is the imaginary number $i = \sqrt{-1}$. The expression $\cos x + i \sin x$ can be written cis x, making the formula appear in the format $z^n = r^n$ cis nx.

Note that De Moivre's theorem is only for angles in polar form. If you are given an angle in degrees, you must convert to polar form before using the formula.

PRACTICE

P1. Convert the following angles from degrees to radians:

(a) 56°

(b) 12°

(c) 199°

P2. Convert the following angles from radians to degrees:

(a) 3

(b) 3π

(c) 33

P3. Simplify the following trigonometric expressions:

(a) $\dfrac{\sin x \tan x + \cos x}{\sec x}$

(b) $\dfrac{4 \cos 2x}{\sin^2 2x} + \sec^2 x$

PRACTICE SOLUTIONS

P1. Multiply each by the conversion factor $\frac{\pi}{180°}$:

(a) $56° \times \frac{\pi}{180°} \cong 0.977$

(b) $12° \times \frac{\pi}{180°} \cong 0.209$

(c) $199° \times \frac{\pi}{180°} \cong 3.473$

P2. Multiply each by the conversion factor $\frac{180°}{\pi}$:

(a) $3 \times \frac{180°}{\pi} \cong 171.9°$

(b) $3\pi \times \frac{180°}{\pi} = 540° = 180°$

(c) $33 \times \frac{180°}{\pi} \cong 1890.8° \cong 90.8°$

P3. (a) Utilize trigonometric identities and definitions to simplify. Specifically, $\tan x = \frac{\sin x}{\cos x}$, $\sec x = \frac{1}{\cos x}$, and $\sin^2 x + \cos^2 x = 1$:

$$\frac{\sin x \tan x + \cos x}{\sec x} = \left(\sin x \frac{\sin x}{\cos x} + \cos x\right) \cos x$$
$$= \frac{\sin^2 x}{\cos x} \cos x + \cos^2 x$$
$$= \sin^2 x + \cos^2 x$$
$$= 1$$

(b) Utilize trigonometric identities and definitions to simplify. Specifically, double angle formulas, $\sin^2 x = (\sin x)^2$, and $\sin^2 x + \cos^2 x = 1$:

$$\frac{4 \cos 2x}{\sin^2 2x} + \sec^2 x = \frac{4(\cos^2 x - \sin^2 x)}{4 \sin^2 x \cos^2 x} + \sec^2 x$$
$$= \frac{\cos^2 x - \sin^2 x}{\sin^2 x \cos^2 x} + \sec^2 x$$
$$= \frac{\cos^2 x}{\sin^2 x \cos^2 x} - \frac{\sin^2 x}{\sin^2 x \cos^2 x} + \sec^2 x$$
$$= \frac{1}{\sin^2 x} - \frac{1}{\cos^2 x} + \sec^2 x$$
$$= \csc^2 x - \sec^2 x + \sec^2 x$$
$$= \csc^2 x$$

48

FTCE Practice Test

Number Sense and Operations

1. In the base-5 number system, what is the sum of 303 and 2222?

    a. 2030

    b. 2525

    c. 3030

    d. 3530

2. Kim's current monthly rent is $800. She is moving to another apartment complex, where the monthly rent will be $1,100. What is the percent increase in her monthly rent amount?

    a. 25.5%

    b. 27%

    c. 35%

    d. 37.5%

3. Which of the following statements is true?

    a. The set of whole numbers is a subset of the set of natural numbers.

    b. The set of integers is a subset of the set of natural numbers.

    c. The set of integers is a subset of the set of rational numbers.

    d. The set of rational numbers is a subset of the set of integers.

4. Which of the following represents 55 in the base-2 system?

    a. 110

    b. 1101

    c. 101,111

    d. 110,111

5. Marlon pays $45 for a jacket that has been marked down 25%. What was the original cost of the jacket?

    a. $80

    b. $75

    c. $65

    d. $60

6. Which of the following statements is true?

    a. A number is divisible by 6 if the number is divisible by both 2 and 3.

    b. A number is divisible by 4 if the sum of all digits is divisible by 8.

    c. A number is divisible by 3 if the last digit is divisible by 3.

    d. A number is divisible by 7 if the sum of the last two digits is divisible by 7.

7. Which of the following is an irrational number?

    a. $4.\overline{2}$

    b. $\sqrt{2}$

    c. $\dfrac{4}{5}$

    d. $\dfrac{21}{5}$

8. Robert buys a car for $24,210. The price of the car has been marked down by 10%. What was the original price of the car?

    a. $25,900
    b. $26,300
    c. $26,900
    d. $27,300

9. Carlos spends $\frac{1}{8}$ of his monthly salary on utility bills. If his utility bills total $320, what is his monthly salary?

    a. $2,440
    b. $2,520
    c. $2,560
    d. $2,600

10. Which of the following is closed under the operation of division?

    a. whole numbers
    b. integers
    c. nonzero rational numbers
    d. irrational numbers

11. Which of the following accurately describes the set of integers?

    a. the set of counting numbers
    b. the set of counting numbers, plus zero
    c. the set of numbers that may be written as the ratio of $\frac{a}{b}$, where b ≠ 0
    d. the set of counting numbers, zero, and the negations of the counting numbers

12. Which of the following correctly compares the sets of rational and irrational numbers?

    a. The set of rational numbers is a subset of the set of irrational numbers.
    b. The set of irrational numbers is a subset of the set of rational numbers.
    c. The sets of irrational and rational numbers are disjoint.
    d. The sets of irrational and rational numbers are equal.

13. Which of the following illustrates the multiplicative inverse property?

    a. The product of a and 1 is a.
    b. The product of $\frac{1}{a}$ and a is 1.
    c. The variable a, raised to the negative 1 power, is equal to the ratio of 1 to a.
    d. The product of a and $-a$ is $-a^2$.

14. For any natural numbers, a, b, and c, assume $a|b$ and $a|c$. Which of the following statements is *not* necessarily true?

    a. $b|c$
    b. $a|(b-c)$
    c. $a|bc$
    d. $a|(b+c)$

15. Which of the following equations may be used to convert $0.\overline{4}$ to a fraction?

a. $10x - x = 4.\overline{4} - 0.\overline{4}$
b. $100x - x = 4.\overline{4} - 0.\overline{4}$
c. $10x - x = 44.\overline{4} - 4.\overline{4}$
d. $100x - 10x = 4.\overline{4} - 0.\overline{4}$

16. Jason decides to donate 1% of his annual salary to a local charity. If his annual salary is $45,000, how much will he donate?

a. $4.50
b. $45
c. $450
d. $4,500

17. Kendra uses the pie chart below to represent the allocation of her annual income. Her annual income is $40,000.

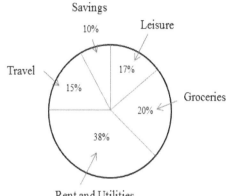

Which of the following statements is true?

a. The amount of money she spends on travel and savings is more than $11,000.
b. The amount of money she spends on rent and utilities is approximately $15,000.
c. The amount of money she spends on groceries and savings is more than $13,000.
d. The amount of money she spends on leisure is less than $5,000.

18. Which of the following correctly represents the expanded form of 0.867?

a. $8 \times \frac{1}{10^0} + 6 \times \frac{1}{10^1} + 7 \times \frac{1}{10^2}$
b. $8 \times \frac{1}{10^2} + 6 \times \frac{1}{10^3} + 7 \times \frac{1}{10^4}$
c. $8 \times \frac{1}{10^3} + 6 \times \frac{1}{10^2} + 7 \times \frac{1}{10^1}$
d. $8 \times \frac{1}{10^1} + 6 \times \frac{1}{10^2} + 7 \times \frac{1}{10^3}$

19. Which expression is represented by the diagram below?

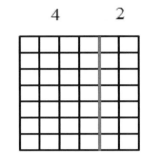

a. $7 + (4 + 2)$
b. $7 \times (4 \times 2)$
c. $7 + (4 \times 2)$
d. $7 \times (4 + 2)$

20. $b|a$ if

a. $a = b \times q$
b. $a = b + q$
c. $b = a \times q$
d. $b = a + q$

21. Which of the following sets is *not* closed under subtraction?

a. integers
b. real numbers
c. natural numbers
d. rational numbers

22. A dress is marked down 45%. The cost, after taxes, is $39.95. If the tax rate is 8.75%, what was the original price of the dress?

a. $45.74
b. $58.61
c. $66.79
d. $72.31

23. Amy saves $450 every 3 months. How much does she save after 3 years?

a. $4,800
b. $5,200
c. $5,400
d. $5,800

24. The table below shows the average amount of rainfall Houston receives during the summer and autumn months.

Month	Amount of Rainfall (in inches)
June	5.35
July	3.18
August	3.83
September	4.33
October	4.5
November	4.19

What percentage of rainfall received during this timeframe, is received during the month of October?

    a. 13.5%
    b. 15.1%
    c. 16.9%
    d. 17.7%

25. Which of the following represents 30,490?

    a. 3.049×10^{-4}
    b. 3.049×10^{3}
    c. 30.490×10^{3}
    d. 3.049×10^{4}

Algebra and Functions

26. Which of the following formulas may be used to represent the sequence 1, 2, 4, 8, 16, ...?

    a. $y = 2x$
    b. $y = x + 2$
    c. $y = 2^{x-1}$
    d. $y = x^{2}$

27. Which of the following formulas may be used to represent the sequence 8, 13, 18, 23, 28, ...?

    a. $a_n = 5n + 3; n \in \mathbb{N}$
    b. $a_n = n + 5; n \in \mathbb{N}$
    c. $a_n = n + 8; n \in \mathbb{N}$
    d. $a_n = 5n + 8; n \in \mathbb{N}$

28. Which of the following graphs does *not* represent a function?

a.

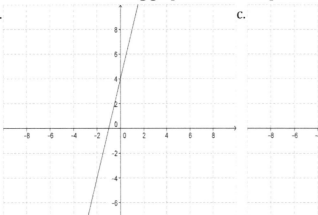

c.

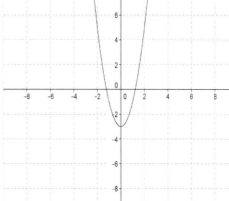

b.

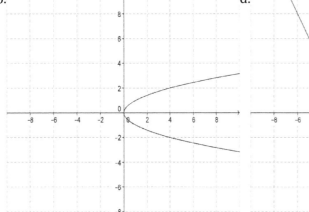

d.

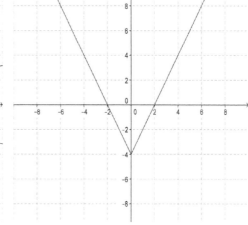

29. Which of the following represents a proportional relationship?

a.

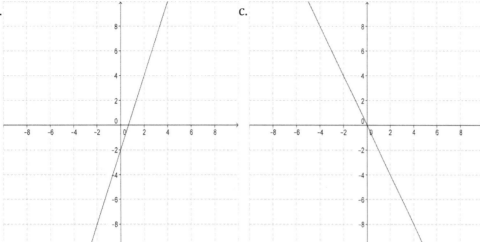

b.

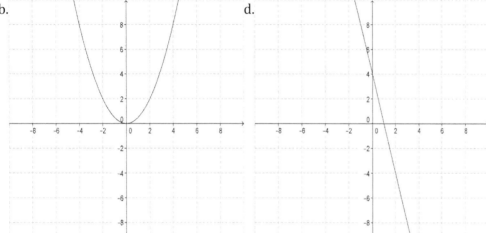

30. Which of the following represents the graph of $y = (x - 4)^2 + 3$?

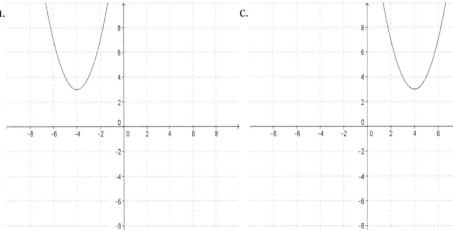

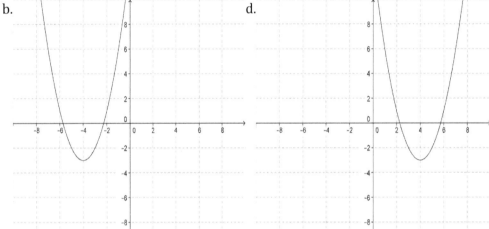

31. The expression $2x^2 - 4x - 30$ is equal to the product of $(x - 5)$ and which other factor?

a. $(2x - 10)$
b. $(2x + 25)$
c. $(2x + 7)$
d. $(2x + 6)$

32. What is the constant of proportionality represented by the table below?

x	y
2	−8
5	−20
7	−28
10	−40
11	−44

a. −12
b. −8
c. −6
d. −4

56

33. Which of the following represents an inverse proportional relationship?

a. $y = 3x$

b. $y = \frac{1}{3}x$

c. $y = \frac{3}{x}$

d. $y = 3x^2$

34. Which of the following expressions is equivalent to $-3x(x-2)^2$?

a. $-3x^3 + 6x^2 - 12x$

b. $-3x^3 - 12x^2 + 12x$

c. $-3x^2 + 6x$

d. $-3x^3 + 12x^2 - 12x$

35. Which of the following graphs represents the solution to $y \geq 3x - 6$?

a. 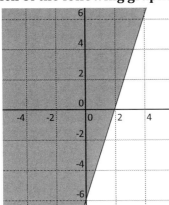 c.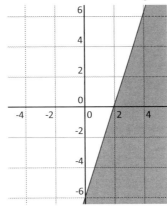

b. 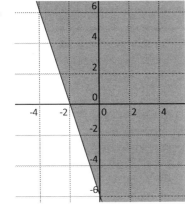 d.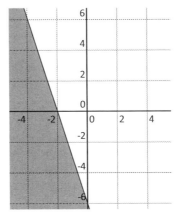

36. If $f(x) = \frac{x^3 - 2x + 1}{3x}$, what is $f(2)$?

a. $\frac{1}{3}$

b. $\frac{1}{2}$

c. $\frac{5}{6}$

d. $\frac{5}{2}$

37. The variables x and y are in a linear relationship. The table below shows a few sample values. Which of the following graphs correctly represents the linear equation relating x and y?

x	y
−2	−11
−1	−8
0	−5
1	−2
2	1

a.

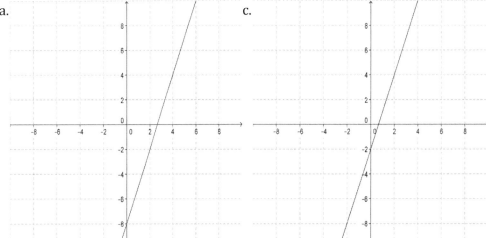

c.

b.

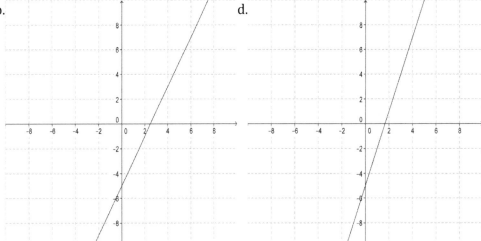

d.

38. Which of the following is the graph of the equation $y = -4x - 6$?

a.

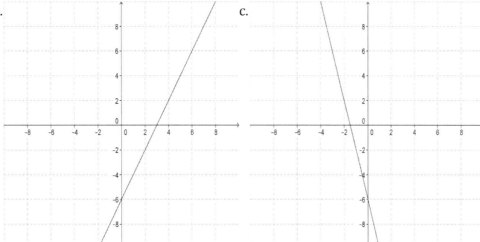

c.

b.

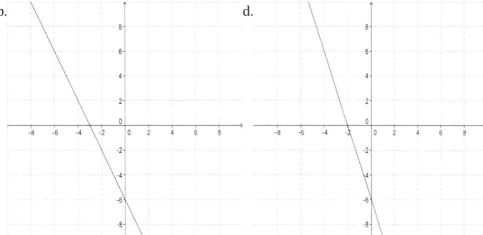

d.

39. Given the graph below, what is the average rate of change from f(2) to f(5)?

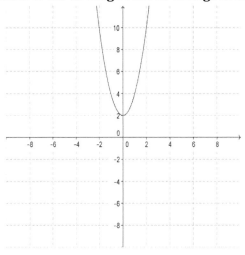

a. 2
b. 14
c. 21
d. 42

40. Elijah pays a $30 park entrance fee, plus $4 for every ticket purchased. Which of the following equations represents the cost?

a. $y = 30x + 4$
b. $y = 34x$
c. $y = 4x + 30$
d. $y = 34x + 30$

41. What is the solution to the system of linear equations graphed below?

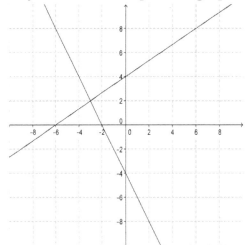

a. $(2, -3)$
b. $(-3, -2)$
c. $(-2, 3)$
d. $(-3, 2)$

60

42. What is the solution to the system of linear equations below?

$$4x - 2y = -38$$
$$2x + 3y = 17$$

a. $(-5, 9)$
b. $(-2, 11)$
c. $(-3, 7)$
d. $(-4, 11)$

43. Which of the following graphs represents the solution to the system of inequalities below?

$$2x - 3y \geq -11$$
$$-2x + 4y \geq 14$$

a.
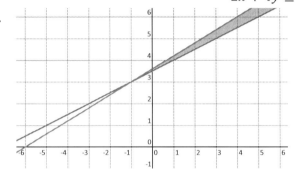

c.
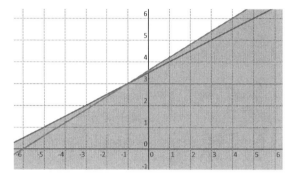

b.
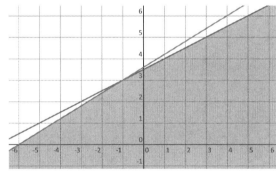

d.
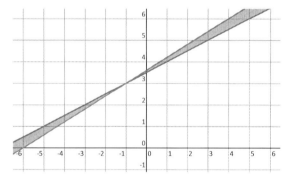

44. Robert drops a ball from his balcony. The height of the ball is modeled by the function $f(x) = -2x^2 + x + 11$, where $f(x)$ represents the height of the ball and x represents the number of seconds. Which of the following best represents the number of seconds that will pass before the ball reaches the ground?

a. 1.4
b. 1.9
c. 2.1
d. 2.6

45. Which type of function is represented by the table of values below?

x	y
−2	0.25
−1	0.5
0	1
1	2
2	4

a. linear
b. quadratic
c. cubic
d. exponential

46. What linear equation includes the data in the table below?

x	y
−3	1
1	−11
3	−17
5	−23
9	−35

a. $y = -3x - 11$
b. $y = -6x - 8$
c. $y = -3x - 8$
d. $y = -12x - 11$

47. Which of the following equations represents a line perpendicular to the one graphed below and passing through the point $(3, 2)$?

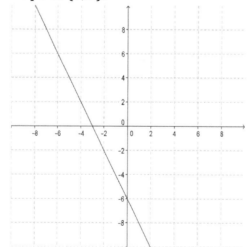

a. $y = \frac{1}{2}x + 2$
b. $y = \frac{1}{2}x + \frac{1}{2}$
c. $y = \frac{3}{2}x + \frac{1}{2}$
d. $y = 2x + 2$

48. Which of the following equations represents a line parallel to the one graphed below and passing through the point $(-1, 4)$?

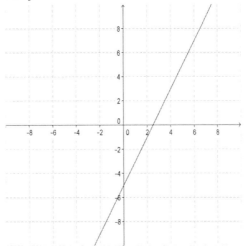

a. $y = 2x - 2$
b. $y = 3x + 6$
c. $y = 3x - 4$
d. $y = 2x + 6$

49. Hannah's monthly gym membership cost is represented by the graph shown below. Which of the following statements is correct?

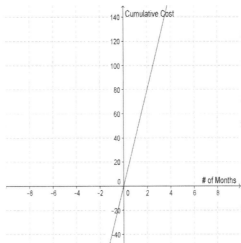

a. The cost is linear, but not proportional.
b. The cost is linear and proportional.
c. The cost is proportional, but not linear.
d. The cost represents an inverse proportional relationship.

50. Amanda saves $0.02 during Month 1. During each subsequent month, she plans to save twice as much as she did the previous month. Which of the following equations represents the amount she will save during the nth month?

    a. $a_n = 0.02 \times 2^{n-1}$
    b. $a_n = 0.02 + 2^n$
    c. $a_n = 0.02 \times 2^n$
    d. $a_n = 2n - 1.98$

51. Kevin saves $3 during Month 1. During each subsequent month, he plans to save 4 more dollars than he saved during the previous month. Which of the following equations represents the amount he will save during the nth month?

    a. $a_n = 3n - 1$
    b. $a_n = 3n + 4$
    c. $a_n = 4n + 3$
    d. $a_n = 4n - 1$

52. What is $\lim\limits_{n \to \infty} \frac{n^2+1}{n}$?

    a. 0
    b. 1
    c. 2
    d. There is no limit.

53. What is $\lim\limits_{n \to \infty} \frac{5n+2}{n}$?

    a. 0
    b. 2
    c. 5
    d. There is no limit.

54. The initial term of a sequence is 3. Each term in the sequence is $\frac{2}{3}$ the amount of the previous term. What is the sum of the terms, as n approaches infinity?

    a. 6
    b. 9
    c. 12
    d. 15

55. Mandy can buy 4 containers of yogurt and 3 boxes of crackers for $9.55. She can buy 2 containers of yogurt and 2 boxes of crackers for $5.90. How much does one box of crackers cost?

    a. $1.75
    b. $2.00
    c. $2.25
    d. $2.50

56. What is the derivative of $f(x) = 9x^2$?

    a. $3x$
    b. $9x$
    c. 18x
    d. $18x^2$

57. Which of the following functions converges?

a. $f(x) = \dfrac{x^2}{x}$

b. $f(x) = 2x$

c. $f(x) = \dfrac{4x}{x} + 1000$

d. $f(x) = \dfrac{3x^2 + 100}{x}$

58. McKenzie shades $\dfrac{1}{5}$ of a piece of paper. Then, she shades an additional area $\dfrac{1}{5}$ the size of what she just shaded. Next, she shades another area $\dfrac{1}{5}$ as large as the previous one. As she continues the process to infinity, what is the limit of the shaded fraction of the paper?

a. $\dfrac{1}{5}$

b. $\dfrac{1}{4}$

c. $\dfrac{1}{3}$

d. $\dfrac{1}{2}$

59. Which of the following functions has a limit of 0?

a. $f(x) = 2x$

b. $f(x) = \dfrac{4}{x}$

c. $f(x) = \dfrac{x}{8}$

d. $f(x) = \dfrac{3x + 1}{x}$

60. What is the derivative of $g(x) = x^{ab}$?

a. $ab \times x^{ab}$

b. $ab \times x^{ab-1}$

c. $a \times x^{ab}$

d. $b \times x^{ab-1}$

61. Which of the following graphs represents an inverse proportional relationship?

a.
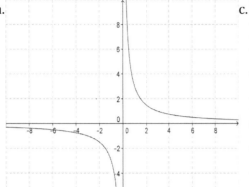

c.
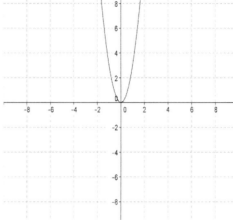

b.
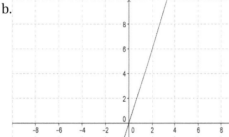

d.
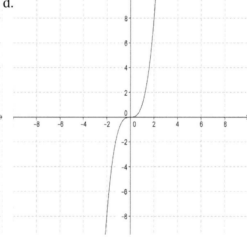

62. What is the sum of the first 50 even, positive integers?

a. 1,250
b. 2,025
c. 2,550
d. 3,250

63. The graph of the parent function $y = x^2$ is shifted 5 units to the left and 4 units down. Which of the following equations represents the transformed function?

a. $y = (x - 5)^2 - 4$
b. $y = (x + 5)^2 - 4$
c. $y = (x - 5)^2 + 4$
d. $y = (x + 5)^2 + 4$

64. Which of the following represents a function?

a. $\{(2, 9), (3, 4), (6, 8), (-1, 5), (3, -1)\}$
b. $\{(8, 7), (7, 9), (2, 1), (4, 3), (3, 6)\}$
c. $\{(-4, 6), (2, 1), (-4, -2), (3, 8), (9, 2)\}$
d. $\{(2, 6), (6, 5), (5, 9), (2, 0), (-3, 1)\}$

66

65. A car is accelerated. Which of the following accurately describes the appearance of the position-time graph?

    a. It is a line with a positive slope.
    b. It is a line with a negative slope.
    c. It is a curve with an increasing slope.
    d. It is a curve with a decreasing slope.

66. Tom needs to buy ink cartridges and printer paper. Each ink cartridge costs $30. Each ream of paper costs $5. He has $100 to spend. Which of the following inequalities may be used to find the combinations of ink cartridges and printer paper that he may purchase?

    a. $30c + 5p \leq 100$
    b. $30c + 5p < 100$
    c. $30c + 5p > 100$
    d. $30c + 5p \geq 100$

67. Hannah spends at least $16 on 4 packages of coffee. Which of the following inequalities represents the possible costs?

    a. $16 \geq 4p$
    b. $16 < 4p$
    c. $16 > 4p$
    d. $16 \leq 4p$

68. $f(x) = \frac{x+1}{2x}$. **What is the equation of the horizontal asymptote?**

    a. $y = \frac{1}{4}$
    b. $y = \frac{1}{2}$
    c. $y = 0$
    d. $y = 2$

69. $g(x) = \frac{x}{x+3}$. **What is the equation of the horizontal asymptote?**

    a. $y = 0$
    b. $y = 0.5$
    c. $y = 1$
    d. $y = 3$

70. What is $\lim\limits_{x \to -\infty} \frac{4x^2}{x+2}$?

    a. -4000
    b. -400
    c. 0
    d. There is no limit.

71. What is $\lim\limits_{x \to -2} (3x^3 - 6x^2 + 4)$?

    a. -44
    b. -42
    c. 4
    d. 52

72. Jackson can decorate a cake in 3 hours. Eli can decorate the same cake in 2 hours. If they work together, how long will it take them to decorate the cake?

    a. 0.8 hours

    b. 1.2 hours

    c. 1.5 hours

    d. 1.8 hours

73. Robert needs to buy milk and bread. Each gallon of milk costs $3. Each loaf of bread costs $2. He intends to spend at least $20. Which of the following graphs represents the possible combinations of gallons of milk and loaves of bread that he may purchase?

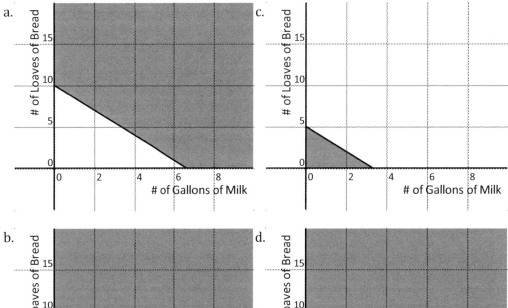

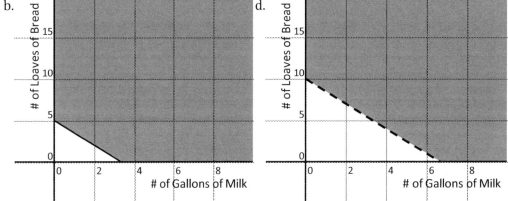

74. Kayla has a $75 budget to purchase gifts for her colleagues. She wants to buy coffee mugs and note pads. She may purchase a maximum of 30 items. Each coffee mug costs $6 and each note pad costs $3. Which of the following graphs correctly shows the possible combinations of coffee mugs and note pads that she may buy?

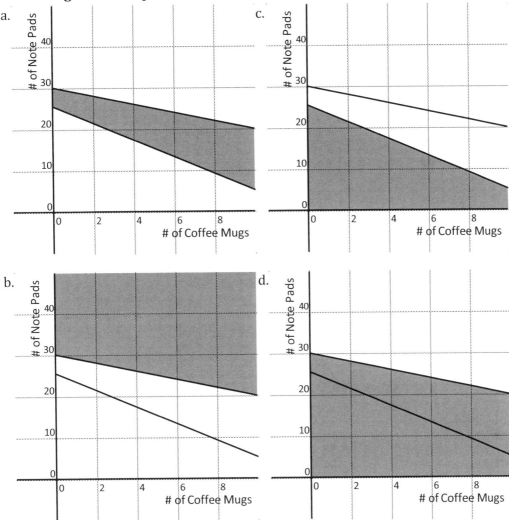

75. Which of the following tables contains points in an exponential function?

a.

x	y
-2	-24
1	12
3	36
5	60
8	96

c.

x	y
-1	-1
1	1
3	27
5	125
6	216

b.

x	y
-2	12
0	0
2	12
4	48
6	108

d.

x	y
-1	0.5
0	1
3	8
5	32
6	64

69

Measurement and Geometry

76. A city is at an elevation of 6,700 feet. Which of the following best represents the elevation in miles?

    a. 0.77 miles
    b. 1.27 miles
    c. 1.56 miles
    d. 1.89 miles

77. A can has a radius of 1.5 inches and a height of 3 inches. Which of the following best represents the volume of the can?

    a. 17.2 in^3
    b. 19.4 in^3
    c. 21.2 in^3
    d. 23.4 in^3

78. A ball has a diameter of 7 inches. Which of the following best represents the volume?

    a. 165.7 in^3
    b. 179.6 in^3
    c. 184.5 in^3
    d. 192.3 in^3

79. A gift box has a length of 14 inches, a height of 8 inches, and a width of 6 inches. How many square inches of wrapping paper are needed to wrap the box?

    a. 56
    b. 244
    c. 488
    d. 672

80. Aidan has a plastic container in the shape of a square pyramid. He wants to fill the container with chocolate candies. If the base has a side length of 6 inches and the height of the container is 9 inches, how many cubic inches of space may be filled with candies?

    a. 98
    b. 102
    c. 108
    d. 112

81. Eric has a beach ball with a radius of 9 inches. He is planning to wrap the ball with wrapping paper. Which of the following is the best estimate for the number of square feet of wrapping paper he will need?

    a. 4.08
    b. 5.12
    c. 7.07
    d. 8.14

82. Each base of a triangular prism has a base length of 9 cm and a height of 12 cm. The height of the prism is 15 cm. What is the volume of the prism?

    a. 652 cm³
    b. 720 cm³
    c. 792 cm³
    d. 810 cm³

83. The two prisms shown below are similar. What is the measurement of *x*?

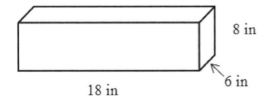 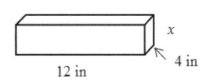

    a. $4\frac{3}{4}$ in
    b. $5\frac{1}{3}$ in
    c. $5\frac{2}{3}$ in
    d. $5\frac{3}{4}$ in

84. Given that the two horizontal lines in the diagram below are parallel, which pair of angles is congruent?

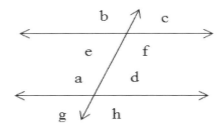

    a. ∠e and ∠b
    b. ∠d and ∠h
    c. ∠g and ∠c
    d. ∠d and ∠f

85. Given the diagram below, which of the following theorems may be used to verify that lines *a* and *b* are parallel?

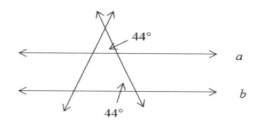

    a. Alternate Interior Angles Converse Theorem
    b. Alternate Exterior Angles Converse Theorem
    c. Consecutive Interior Angles Converse Theorem
    d. Corresponding Angles Converse Theorem

86. Given the diagram below, what is the measure of the inscribed angle?

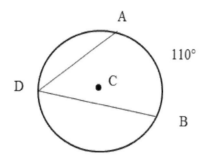

    a. 37°
    b. 45°
    c. 55°
    d. 57°

87. A tree with a height of 15 feet casts a shadow that is 5 feet in length. A man standing at the base of the shadow formed by the tree is 6 feet tall. How long is the shadow cast by the man?

    a. 1.5 feet
    b. 2 feet
    c. 2.5 feet
    d. 3 feet

88. Which of the following best represents the measurement of x, shown in the triangle below?

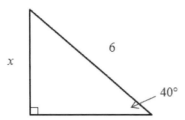

a. 2.6
b. 3.1
c. 3.9
d. 4.4

89. What is the area of the shaded region in the figure shown below?

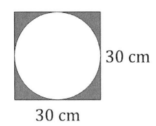

30 cm

30 cm

a. 177 cm^2
b. 181 cm^2
c. 187 cm^2
d. 193 cm^2

90. Which of the following postulates proves the congruence of the triangles below?

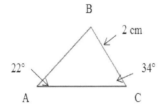 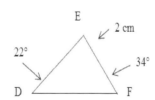

a. ASA
b. AAS
c. SAS
d. SSS

91. A man standing on a flat, level surface casts a shadow that is 6.2 ft in length. The man is 5.8 ft tall. Which of the following best represents the distance from the top of his head to the end of the shadow?

    a. 7 ft
    b. 7.5 ft
    c. 8 ft
    d. 8.5 ft

92. A cylindrical carrot stick is sliced with a knife. Which of the following shapes is *not* a possible cross-section?

    a. circle
    b. rectangle
    c. ellipse
    d. triangle

93. What is the value of x, shown in the diagram below?

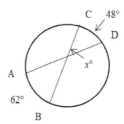

    a. 16
    b. 24
    c. 48
    d. 55

94. What is the value of x, shown in the diagram below?

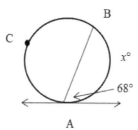

    a. 68°
    b. 76°
    c. 128°
    d. 136°

95. Which of the following represents the net of a triangular prism?

a.   c.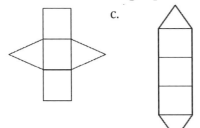

b.   d.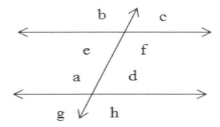

96. A convex three-dimensional figure has 9 edges and 6 vertices. How many faces does it have?

 a. 4
 b. 5
 c. 6
 d. 8

97. Given that the two horizontal lines in the diagram below are parallel, which of the following statements is correct?

 a. ∠b and ∠g are complementary.
 b. ∠d and ∠c are supplementary.
 c. ∠a and ∠e are supplementary.
 d. ∠e and ∠h are congruent.

98. Which of the following postulates may be used to prove the similarity of △ABC and △ADE?

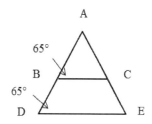

a. ASA
b. AA
c. SAS
d. SSS

99. Which of the following transformations has been applied to △ABC?

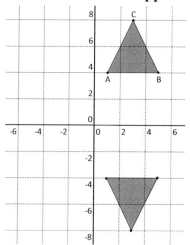

a. translation
b. rotation of 90 degrees
c. reflection
d. dilation

100. Which of the following steps were applied to △*ABC*?

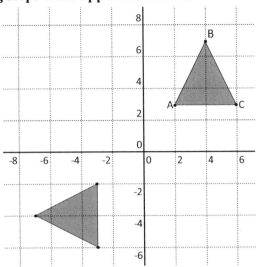

    a. reflection across the *x*-axis and rotation of 90 degrees
    b. reflection across the *x*-axis and rotation of 180 degrees
    c. reflection across the *x*-axis and rotation of 270 degrees
    d. reflection across the *y*-axis and rotation of 180 degrees

101. What is the midpoint of the line segment below?

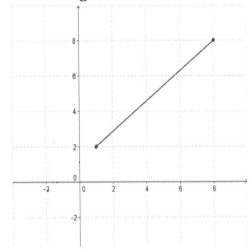

    a. $(3.5, 4)$
    b. $(4, 4)$
    c. $(4.5, 5)$
    d. $(5, 5)$

102. What is the distance on a coordinate plane from $(-8, 6)$ to $(4, 3)$?

    a. $\sqrt{139}$
    b. $\sqrt{147}$
    c. $\sqrt{153}$
    d. $\sqrt{161}$

103. What is the perimeter of the trapezoid graphed below?

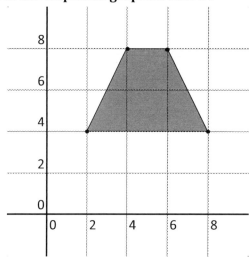

a. $4 + \sqrt{10}$
b. $8 + 4\sqrt{5}$
c. $4 + 2\sqrt{5}$
d. $8 + 2\sqrt{22}$

104. What is the area of the figure graphed below?

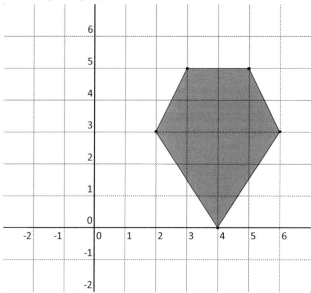

a. 11 units^2
b. 11.5 units^2
c. 12 units^2
d. 12.5 units^2

105. What scale factor was applied to the larger triangle to obtain the smaller triangle below?

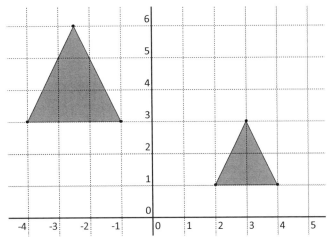

a. $\dfrac{1}{4}$

b. $\dfrac{1}{3}$

c. $\dfrac{1}{2}$

d. $\dfrac{2}{3}$

106. Which of the following pairs of equations represents the lines of symmetry in the figure below?

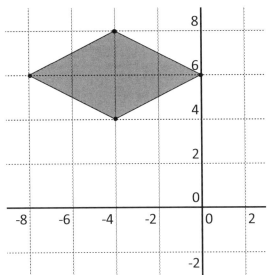

a. $x = -4, y = 6$

b. $x = 4, y = 6$

c. $y = -4, x = 6$

d. $y = 4, x = -6$

107. Which of the following pairs of shapes may tessellate a plane?

    a. regular pentagons and squares
    b. regular pentagons and equilateral triangles
    c. equilateral triangles and regular hexagons
    d. regular octagons and equilateral triangles

108. Andrea must administer $\frac{1}{12}$ of a medicine bottle to a patient. If the bottle contains $3\frac{4}{10}$ fluid ounces of medicine, how much medicine should be administered?

    a. $\frac{17}{60}$ fluid ounces
    b. $\frac{15}{62}$ fluid ounces
    c. $\frac{3}{19}$ fluid ounces
    d. $\frac{17}{67}$ fluid ounces

109. What is the slope of the leg marked x in the triangle graphed below?

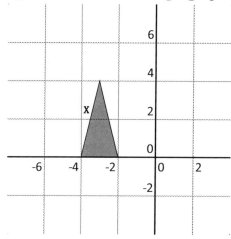

    a. 2
    b. 3.5
    c. 4
    d. 4.5

110. Ann must walk from Point A to Point B and then to Point C. Finally, she will walk back to Point A. If each unit represents 5 miles, which of the following best represents the total distance she will have walked?

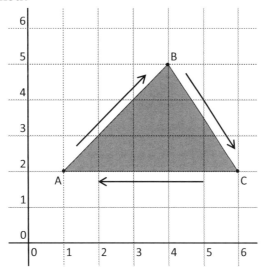

a. 42 miles
b. 48 miles
c. 56 miles
d. 64 miles

111. Which of the following measurements is the best approximation of 2,012 square inches?

a. 11.85 ft^2
b. 12.28 ft^2
c. 13.97 ft^2
d. 15.29 ft^2

112. What is the length of the hypotenuse in the triangle shown below?

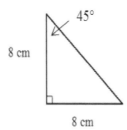

a. 4 cm
b. $8\sqrt{3}$ cm
c. 16 cm
d. $8\sqrt{2}$ cm

Statistics, Probability, and Discrete Mathematics

113. For which of the following data sets would the mean be an appropriate measure of center to use?

    a. 7, 15, 20, 24, 27, 28, 31, 36, 41, 50
    b. 6, 7, 8, 8, 9, 9, 10, 20, 34, 50
    c. 5, 18, 30, 42, 43, 44, 46, 48, 49, 50
    d. 8, 10, 12, 13, 14, 16, 20, 22, 24, 2200

114. A student scores 82 on a final exam. The class average is 87, with a standard deviation of 2 points. How many standard deviations below the class average is the student's score?

    a. 1.5
    b. 2
    c. 2.5
    d. 3

115. A student scores 61 on a test. The class average is 81, with a standard deviation of 10 points. What percentage of the class scored below this student?

    a. 1.26%
    b. 1.43%
    c. 1.96%
    d. 2.28%

116. A student scores 96 on a test. The class average is 84, with a standard deviation of 4 points. What percentage of the class scored below this student?

    a. 78.89%
    b. 82.77%
    c. 92.67%
    d. 99.87%

117. A student scores 68 on a final exam. Another student scores 84 on the exam. The class average is 80, with a standard deviation of 8 points. What percentage of the class scored within the range of these two students' scores?

    a. 44.32%
    b. 48.54%
    c. 58.39%
    d. 62.47%

118. Class A, with a total of 28 students, had a final exam average of 85 and a standard deviation of 4.5 points. Class B, with a total of 30 students, had a final exam average of 88, with a standard deviation of 4 points. Which of the following statements is true?

    a. There is no significant difference between the classes, as evidenced by a p-value greater than 0.05.
    b. There is no significant difference between the classes, as evidenced by a p-value less than 0.05.
    c. There is a significant difference between the classes, as evidenced by a p-value greater than 0.05.
    d. There is a significant difference between the classes, as evidenced by a p-value less than 0.05.

119. A beverage manufacturer claims to include 20 ounces in each bottle. A random sample of 30 bottles shows a mean of 19.8 ounces, with a standard deviation of 0.2 ounces. Which of the following statements is correct?

    a. The manufacturer's claim is likely true, as evidenced by a p-value less than 0.01.
    b. The manufacturer's claim is likely true, as evidenced by a p-value greater than 0.01.
    c. The manufacturer's claim is likely false, as evidenced by a p-value less than 0.01.
    d. The manufacturer's claim is likely false, as evidenced by a p-value greater than 0.01.

120. An oatmeal manufacturer claims to include 18 ounces in each container, with a standard deviation of 0.3 ounces. A random sample of 25 containers shows a mean of 17.9 ounces. Which of the following statements is true?

    a. The manufacturer's claim is likely true, as evidenced by a p-value less than 0.05.
    b. The manufacturer's claim is likely true, as evidenced by a p-value greater than 0.05.
    c. The manufacturer's claim is likely false, as evidenced by a p-value less than 0.05.
    d. The manufacturer's claim is likely false, as evidenced by a p-value greater than 0.05.

121. A professor claims that the average on his final exam is 82. A random sample of 30 students shows an exam mean of 83 and a standard deviation of 2 points. Which of the following statements is true?

    a. The professor's claim is likely true, as evidenced by a p-value less than 0.05.
    b. The professor's claim is likely false, as evidenced by a p-value less than 0.05.
    c. The professor's claim is likely true, as evidenced by a p-value greater than 0.05.
    d. The professor's claim is likely false, as evidenced by a p-value greater than 0.05.

122. Which of the following describes a sampling technique that will likely increase the sampling error?

    a. choosing every 5th person from a list
    b. grouping a sample according to gender and then choosing every 10th person from a list
    c. using an intact group
    d. assigning numbers to a sample and then using a random number generator to choose numbers

123. What is the area under the normal curve between ±2 standard deviations?

    a. approximately 68%
    b. approximately 90%
    c. approximately 95%
    d. approximately 99%

124. Which of the following best represents the standard deviation of the data below?

      3, 4, 4, 5, 6, 12, 12, 15

    a. 2.9
    b. 3.4
    c. 4.1
    d. 4.6

125. Given the boxplots below, which of the following statements is correct?

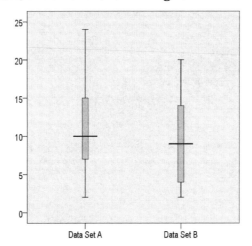

Data Set A   Data Set B

a. Data Set A has a larger range and a larger median.
b. Data Set A has a smaller range and a larger median.
c. Data Set A has a larger range and a smaller median.
d. Data Set A has a smaller range and a smaller median.

126. What is the interquartile range of the data below?

 2, 4, 6, 8, 10, 12, 14, 16, 18, 20

a. 10
b. 11
c. 12
d. 13

127. According to the scatter plot below, which of the following is the *best* estimate for the earnings received for 20 hours of work?

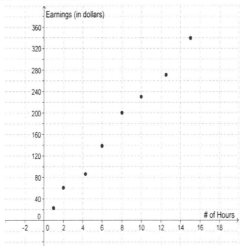

a. $342
b. $446
c. $528
d. $602

128. Which of the following statements is *not* true?

    a. In a skewed distribution, the mean is pulled towards the tail.

    b. In a skewed distribution, the mean is pulled towards the area with a higher frequency of scores.

    c. In a normal distribution, the mean, median, and mode are the same value.

    d. The area under a normal curve is 1.

129. Given the two-way frequency table below, which of the following *best* represents P(male or graduate)?

	Undergraduate	Graduate	Total
Male	2940	2045	4985
Female	3026	2068	5094
Total	5966	4113	10,079

    a. 55%

    b. 60%

    c. 70%

    d. 75%

130. Adam rolls a standard six-sided die. What is the probability he rolls a number greater than or equal to 5?

    a. $\frac{1}{6}$

    b. $\frac{1}{5}$

    c. $\frac{1}{4}$

    d. $\frac{1}{3}$

131. Kayla rolls a die and tosses a coin. What is the probability she gets an even number and heads?

    a. $\frac{1}{6}$

    b. $\frac{1}{4}$

    c. $\frac{1}{3}$

    d. 1

132. Eli rolls a die and tosses a coin. What is the probability he gets a prime number or tails?

    a. $\frac{1}{2}$

    b. $\frac{2}{3}$

    c. $\frac{3}{4}$

    d. $\frac{5}{6}$

133. Andrew rolls a die. What is the probability he gets a 4 or an even number?

    a. $\frac{1}{4}$

    b. $\frac{1}{2}$

    c. $\frac{2}{3}$

    d. $\frac{3}{4}$

134. The simulation of a coin toss is completed 300 times. Which of the following best represents the number of tosses you can expect to show heads?

    a. 50

    b. 100

    c. 150

    d. 200

135. How many ways can you arrange the letters below, if order does not matter?
HANNAH

    a. 30

    b. 60

    c. 90

    d. 120

136. How many ways can 1st – 3rd place winners be chosen from 6 people?

    a. 120

    b. 60

    c. 30

    d. 20

137. How many ways can the numerals 0 – 9 be arranged?

    a. 36,045

    b. 182,492

    c. 1,048,644

    d. 3,628,800

138. What is the limit of the series below?

$$1 + \frac{1}{2} + \frac{1}{4} + \frac{1}{8} + \frac{1}{16} + \cdots$$

    a. 2

    b. $2\frac{1}{4}$

    c. $2\frac{3}{4}$

    d. 3

139. What is the size of the sample space for tossing four coins?

    a. 8

    b. 12

    c. 16

    d. 20

140. 320 students are surveyed. 120 of the students like only Dallas. 150 of the students like only Houston. 48 of the students like neither city. How many students like Dallas *and* Houston?

a. 2
b. 3
c. 4
d. 5

141. $A = \{5, 9, 2, 3, -1, 8\}$ and $B = \{2, 0, 4, 5, 6, 8\}$. What is $A \cap B$?

a. $\{5, 2, 8\}$
b. $\{-1, 0, 2, 3, 4, 5, 6, 8, 9\}$
c. $\emptyset$
d. $\{5, 8\}$

142. $A = \{9, 4, -3, 8, 6, 0\}$ and $B = \{-4, 2, 8, 9, 0\}$. What is $A \cup B$?

a. $\{9, 8, 0\}$
b. $\{9, 4, -3, 8, 6, 0, -4, 2\}$
c. $\emptyset$
d. $\{9, 8, 0, 2, 4\}$

143. $A = \{3, -4, 1\}$ and $B = \{0, 5, 9, 2\}$. What is $A \cap B$?

a. $\{3, -4, 1, 0, 5, 9, 2\}$
b. $\{-4, 2, 3\}$
c. $\{0, 1, 2, 3, 5, 9\}$
d. $\emptyset$

144. What is the contrapositive of the statement below?

If I get paid, then I go to the beach.

a. If I get paid, then I do not go to the beach.
b. If I go to the beach, then I get paid.
c. If I do not get paid, then I go to the beach.
d. If I do not go to the beach, then I do not get paid.

145. What is the converse of the statement below?

If I go skiing, then it is winter.

a. If it is not winter, then I do not go skiing.
b. If it is winter, then I go skiing.
c. If it is not winter, then I go skiing.
d. If I go skiing, then it is not winter.

146. Using logic, when is $p \vee q$ false?

a. When p is true and q is true.
b. When p is true and q is false.
c. When p is false and q is true.
d. When p is false and q is false.

147. Using logic, when is $p \wedge q$ true?

    a. When p is true and q is true.
    b. When p is true and q is false.
    c. When p is false and q is true.
    d. When p is false and q is false.

148. Which of the following is logically equivalent to $p \rightarrow q$?

    a. $q \rightarrow p$
    b. $\neg p \rightarrow \neg q$
    c. $\neg q \rightarrow \neg p$
    d. $p \wedge q$

149. Eric's dietary plan consists of 4 different entrées, 5 different appetizers, and 3 different desserts. How many possible meals may he create containing one entrée, one appetizer, and one dessert?

    a. 12
    b. 24
    c. 60
    d. 120

150. Which of the following represents a tautology?

    a. $p \wedge \neg p$
    b. $p \vee \neg p$
    c. $p \vee \neg q$
    d. $p \vee q$

Constructed Response

1. A family bought a new car for a purchase price of \$32,000. The car will lose 15% of its value the day it is purchased and the car will depreciate at a constant rate following that. The value of the car as a function of time can be modeled by $y = c - 0.09cx$, where y is the value of the car x years after the car was purchased and c is the value of the car after the initial 15% depreciation.

    a. What is the value of the car 2 years after its purchase date? Show your work.
    b. On an xy-grid, graph the value, y, of the car, as a function of x, where x represents the number of years after the purchase date, for $0 \leq x \leq 7$ years. Label the axes and show the scales used for the graph.
    c. Use your graph to estimate the number of years, x, after the purchase date that the value of the car is \$15,000. Label this point on your graph and indicate the approximate coordinates of the point.
    d. Algebraically find the number of years, x, after the purchase date that the value of the car is exactly \$15,000. Round your solution to the nearest tenth of a year. Show your work.

2. The diagram below shows the plan Berenice has for a triangular splash pad in a local city park. There will be three circles, each with a diameter of 6 feet, and the circles will be enclosed by an equilateral triangle with a side length of 30 feet. Berenice plans to have splash areas/fountains within the circles and walkways in the shaded areas of the triangle.

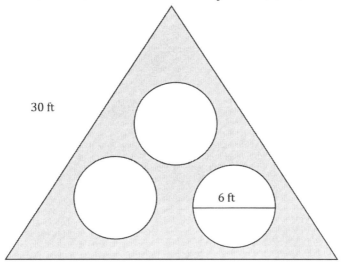

a. According to the diagram, what is the maximum area, in square feet, available for Berenice to have for splash/fountain areas in the triangle? Show your work.

b. According to the diagram, what percentage of the triangle will be set aside for walkways? Show your work.

c. If a ball were to fall on a random point within the triangular splash pad, what is the probability that the ball would fall where Berenice plans to have splash areas? Show your work or explain your reasoning.

3. Below are listed the heights in centimeters of the 19 students in a class.

    48, 53, 53, 54, 55, 56, 59, 60, 60, 63, 63, 63, 64, 65, 66, 67, 69, 71, 73

a. For the numbers above, define and identify the median and the range.

b. Define and calculate the mean for the list of numbers above.

c. Draw a stem and leaf plot of the data using the tens digits as the stems and the units digits as the leaves.

Answer Key and Explanations

Number Sense and Operations

1. C: The sum is written as:

$$\begin{array}{r} 2222 \\ +\ \ 303 \\ \hline 3030 \end{array}$$

The sum of 2 and 3 equals 5, which must be represented as a 10. In the base-5 number system, a number cannot contain any 5's. The 1 of each 10 is carried to the next column to the left.

2. D: The percent increase is represented as $\frac{1100-800}{800}$, which equals 0.375 or 37.5%.

3. C: The set of integers is contained within the set of rational numbers, and is hence, a subset. A rational number may be written as the ratio, $\frac{a}{b}$, where a and b are integers and $b \neq 0$.

4. D: You first divide 2 into 55, recording the remainder. You then divide 2 into each resulting quotient, until the quotient is smaller than 2. Next, you put the final quotient as the first digit. You then go backwards and write the remainders and place them as digits, in order from left to right.

5. D: The original cost may be represented by the equation $45 = x - 0.25x$ or $45 = 0.75x$. Dividing both sides of the equation by 0.75 gives $x = 60$.

6. A: If a number is divisible by 2 and 3, it is also divisible by the lowest common multiple of these two factors. The lowest common multiple of 2 and 3 is their product, 6.

7. B: The decimal expansion of an irrational number does not terminate or repeat. The decimal expansion of $\sqrt{2}$ does not terminate or repeat.

8. C: The original price may be represented by the equation $24,210 = x - 0.10x$ or $24,210 = 0.9x$. Dividing both sides of the equation by 0.9 gives $x = 26,900$.

9. C: His monthly salary may be modeled as $\frac{1}{8}x = 320$. Multiplying both sides of the equation by 8 gives $x = 2,560$.

10. C: Division of a nonzero rational number by another nonzero rational number will always result in a nonzero rational number.

11. D: The set of integers is represented as $\{..., -3, -2, -1, 0, 1, 2, 3, ...\}$. The numbers 1, 2, 3, ..., are counting numbers, or natural numbers. Thus, the set contains the counting numbers, zero, and the negations of the counting numbers.

12. C: The set of irrational numbers is separate from the set of rational numbers. A rational number cannot be irrational, and an irrational number cannot be rational.

13. B: The multiplicative inverse property states: the product of a number and its reciprocal is 1.

14. A: If $a|b$ and $a|c$, it does not necessary follow that $b|c$. One counterexample is $3|6$ and $3|15$, but 6 does not divide 15.

15. A: The repeating decimal may be converted to a fraction by writing:

$$10x = 4.\overline{4}$$
$$- \quad x = 0.\overline{4}$$

which simplifies as $10x - x = 4.\overline{4} - 0.\overline{4}$.

16. C: The amount he donates is equal to $0.01(45,000)$. Thus, he donates \$450.

17. B: The amount she spends on rent and utilities is equal to $0.38(40,000)$, or \$15,200, which is approximately \$15,000.

18. D: The 8 is in the tenths place, the 6 in the hundredths place, and the 7 in the thousandths place. Thus, 0.867 is equal to the sum of the product of 8 and $\frac{1}{10}$, the product of 6 and $\frac{1}{100}$, and the product of 7 and $\frac{1}{1000}$.

19. D: The rectangular array represents the product of the side lengths of 7 and $(4 + 2)$.

20. A: $b|a$ means that a is divisible by b: that is, that a is equal to the product of b and some quotient, q.

21. C: Subtraction of a natural number from another natural number may result in an integer that is not a natural number. For example, $1 - 2 = -1$, which is not a natural number.

22. C: The original price may be modeled by the equation, $(x - 0.45x) + 0.0875(x - 0.45x) = 39.95$, which simplifies to $0.598125x = 39.95$. Dividing each side of the equation by the coefficient of x gives $x \approx 66.79$.

23. C: There are 36 months in 3 years. The following proportion may be written: $\frac{450}{3} = \frac{x}{36}$. The equation $3x = 16,200$, may be solved for x. Dividing both sides of the equation by 3 gives $x = 5,400$.

24. D: The total rainfall is 25.38 inches. Thus, the ratio $\frac{4.5}{25.38}$, represents the percentage of rainfall received during October. $\frac{4.5}{25.38} \approx 0.177$ or 17.7%.

25. D: The decimal point is 4 places to the right of the first digit, 3. Thus, $30,490 = 3.049 \times 10^4$.

Algebra and Functions

26. C: The ratio between successive terms is constant (2), so this is a geometric series. A geometric sequence is represented by an exponential function.

27. A: The sum of 3 and the product of each term number and 5 equals the term value. For example, for term number 4, the value is equal to $5(4) + 3$, or 23.

28. B: A vertical line will cross the graph at more than one point. Thus, it is not a function.

29. C: A proportional relationship is defined as a relationship in which the two variables are always a constant ratio between each other. This effectively means that a proportional relationship has a straight line and that it passes through the origin. One real world example of a proportional relationship is in scaling a recipe. To double a recipe that requires two eggs and one cup of milk, you would multiply both of these values by two to get four eggs and two cups of milk. The ratio of milk to eggs is always 1:2 and could be represented by the graph $y = 2x$. Choices A and D are incorrect because they do not pass through the origin. Choice B is incorrect because it does not maintain a constant ratio between its x-values and y-values.

30. C: This graph is shifted 4 units to the right and 3 units up from that of the parent function, $y = x^2$.

31. D: The product of $(x - 5)(2x + 6)$ equals $2x^2 + 6x - 10x - 30$, which simplifies to $2x^2 - 4x - 30$.

32. D: The constant of proportionality is equal to the slope. Using the points, (2, –8) and (5, –20), the slope may be written as $\frac{-20-(-8)}{5-2}$, which equals –4.

33. C: An inverse proportional relationship is written in the form $y = \frac{k}{x}$, thus the equation $y = \frac{3}{x}$ shows that y is inversely proportional to x.

34. D: The expression $(x - 2)^2$ may be expanded as $x^2 - 4x + 4$. Multiplication of $-3x$ by this expression gives $-3x^3 + 12x^2 - 12x$.

35. A: This graph shows a slope of 3, a y-intercept of –6, and the correct shading above the line. Using the test point (0, 0), the equation $0 \geq 0 - 6$ may be written. Since $0 \geq -6$, the solution is the shaded area above the line, which contains the point (0, 0).

36. C: Substituting 2 for each x-value gives $f(2) = \frac{2^3-2(2)+1}{3(2)}$, which simplifies to $f(2) = \frac{5}{6}$.

37. D: The table shows the y-intercept to be –5. The slope is equal to the ratio of change in y-values to change in corresponding x-values. As each x-value increases by 1, each y-value increases by 3. Thus, the slope is $\frac{3}{1}$, or 3. This graph represents the equation $y = 3x - 5$.

38. C: Each of the graphs shows the correct y-intercept of –6, but only graph C shows the correct slope. Using the points (0, –6) and (–2, 2), the slope of graph C may be written as $m = \frac{2-(-6)}{-2-0}$, which simplifies to $m = -4$.

39. B: The graph shows $f(2) = 10$. Since the y-intercept of the parabola is 2, the following equation may be written: $10 = a(2)^2 + 2$, which simplifies to $10 = 4a + 2$. Subtracting 2 from both sides gives $8 = 4a$. Dividing both sides of the equation by 4 gives $a = 2$. Thus, the graph represents the function, $f(x) = 2x^2 + 2$. Evaluating this function for an x-value of 5 gives $f(5) = 2(5)^2 + 2$ or $f(5) = 52$. The average rate of change may be written as $A(x) = \frac{52-10}{5-2}$, which simplifies to $A(x) = 14$.

40. C: The slope is equal to 4, since each ticket costs $4. The y-intercept is represented by the constant fee of $30. Substituting 4 for m and 30 for b into the equation $y = mx + b$ gives $y = 4x + 30$.

41. D: The lines cross at the point with an x-value of -3 and a y-value of 2. Thus, the solution is $(-3, 2)$.

42. A: On a graph, the lines intersect at the point, $(-5, 9)$. Thus, $(-5, 9)$ is the solution to the system of linear equations.

43. A: The test point of $(0, 0)$ indicates that shading should occur below the line with the steeper slope. The same test point indicates that shading should occur above the other line. The overlapped shading occurs between these two lines, in the upper right.

44. D: A graph of the function shows the positive x-intercept to occur at approximately $(2.6, 0)$. Thus, the ball will reach the ground after approximately 2.6 seconds.

45. D: The table represents a geometric sequence, with a common ratio of 2. Geometric sequences are modeled by exponential functions.

46. C: Using the points $(-3, 1)$ and $(1, -11)$, the slope may be written as $m = \frac{-11-1}{1-(-3)}$ or $m = -3$. Substituting the slope of -3 and the x- and y-values from the point $(-3, 1)$, into the slope-intercept form of an equation gives $1 = -3(-3) + b$, which simplifies to $1 = 9 + b$. Subtracting 9 from both sides of the equation gives $b = -8$. Thus, the linear equation that includes the data in the table is $y = -3x - 8$.

47. B: The slope of the graphed line is -2. A line perpendicular to this one will have a slope of $\frac{1}{2}$. Substituting the slope and the x- and y-values from the point $(3, 2)$, into the slope-intercept form of an equation gives: $2 = \frac{1}{2}(3) + b$, which simplifies to $2 = \frac{3}{2} + b$. Subtracting $\frac{3}{2}$ from each side of the equation gives $b = \frac{1}{2}$. So the equation of a line perpendicular to this one and passing through the point $(3, 2)$ is $y = \frac{1}{2}x + \frac{1}{2}$.

48. D: The slope of the graphed line is 2. A line parallel to this one will also have a slope of 2. Substituting the slope and the x- and y-values from the point $(-1, 4)$, into the slope-intercept form of an equation gives: $4 = 2(-1) + b$, which simplifies to $4 = -2 + b$. Adding 2 to both sides of the equation gives $b = 6$. So the equation of a line parallel to this one and passing through the point $(-1, 4)$ is $y = 2x + 6$.

49. B: The graph is a straight line that passes through the origin, or $(0, 0)$. Thus, it is linear and proportional.

50. A: This situation may be modeled by a geometric sequence, with a common ratio of 2 and initial value of 0.02. Substituting the common ratio and initial value into the formula $a_n = a_1 \times r^{n-1}$, gives $a_n = 0.02 \times 2^{n-1}$.

51. D: This situation may be modeled by an arithmetic sequence, with a common difference of 4 and initial value of 3. Substituting the common difference and initial value into the formula, $a_n = a_1 + (n-1)d$, gives $a_n = 3 + (n-1)4$, which simplifies to $a_n = 4n - 1$.

52. D: If we divide both terms in the numerator by n, the expression reduces to $n + \frac{1}{n}$. Although $\frac{1}{n}$ converges to 0, n increases without bound. The expression therefore has no limit.

53. C: The limit is simply the quotient of $5n$ divided by n, or 5.

54. B: The sum of an infinite geometric series may be modeled by the formula $S = \frac{a}{1-r}$, where a represents the initial value and r represents the common ratio. Substituting the initial value of 3 and common ratio of $\frac{2}{3}$ into the formula, gives $= \frac{3}{1-\frac{2}{3}}$, which simplifies to $S = \frac{3}{\frac{1}{3}}$ or 9.

55. C: The situation may be modeled by the system $\begin{array}{l} 4x + 3y = 9.55 \\ 2x + 2y = 5.90 \end{array}$. Multiplying the bottom equation by -2 gives $\begin{array}{l} 4x + 3y = 9.55 \\ -4x - 4y = -11.80 \end{array}$. Addition of the two equations gives $-y = -2.25$ or $y = 2.25$. Thus, one box of crackers costs $2.25.

56. C: The derivative of an equation of the form $y = ax^n$ is equal to $(n \times a)x^{n-1}$. So the derivative of $y = 9x^2$ is equal to $(2 \times 9)x^{2-1}$ or $18x$.

57. C: The limit of the expression $\frac{4x}{x}$, is 4, so the limit of the entire function is 1,004. The function converges.

58. B: The sequence $\frac{1}{5}, \frac{1}{25}, \frac{1}{125}, \frac{1}{625}, \ldots$, may be used to represent the situation. Substituting the initial value of $\frac{1}{5}$ and common ratio of $\frac{1}{5}$ into the formula $S = \frac{a}{1-r}$ gives $= \frac{\frac{1}{5}}{1-\frac{1}{5}}$, which simplifies to $S = \frac{\frac{1}{5}}{\frac{4}{5}}$ or $S = \frac{1}{4}$.

59. B: As the denominator approaches infinity, the value of the function will get smaller and smaller and converge to 0.

60. B: The derivative of an equation of the form $y = x^n$ is equal to $n \times x^{n-1}$. So the derivative of $g(x) = x^{ab}$ is equal to $ab \times x^{ab-1}$.

61. A: An inverse proportional relationship is represented by an equation in the form $y = \frac{k}{x}$, where k represents some constant of proportionality. The graph of this equation is a hyperbola with diagonal axes, symmetric about the lines $y = x$ and $y = -x$.

62. C: The value of the 50th term may be found using the formula $a_n = a_1 + (n-1)d$. Substituting the number of terms for n, the initial value of 2 for a, and the common difference of 2 for d gives: $a_{50} = 2 + (50-1)(2)$, which simplifies to $a_{50} = 100$. Now, the value of the 50th term may be substituted into the formula, $S_n = \frac{n(a_1+a_n)}{2}$, which gives: $S_{50} = \frac{50(2+100)}{2}$, which simplifies to $S_{50} = 2,550$.

63. B: The sign of the constant, inside the squared term, is positive for a shift to the left and negative for a shift to the right. Thus, a movement of 5 units left is indicated by the expression $y = (x + 5)^2$. A shift of 4 units down is indicated by subtraction of 4 units from the squared term.

64. B: Relation B is the only one in which there is not any x-value that is mapped to more than one y-value. Thus, this relation represents a function.

65. C: The position of an accelerating car is changing according to a non-constant speed. Thus, the graph will show a curve with an increasing slope. The slope is increasing since it represents the velocity, and the velocity is increasing.

66. A: The inequality will be less than or equal to, since he may spend $100 or less on his purchase.

67. D: Since she spends at least \$16, the relation of the number of packages of coffee to the minimum cost may be written as $4p \geq 16$. Alternatively, the inequality may be written as $16 \leq 4p$.

68. B: The horizontal asymptote is equal to the ratio of the coefficient of x to the coefficient of $2x$, or $\frac{1}{2}$.

69. C: The horizontal asymptote is equal to the ratio of the two coefficients of x, or $\frac{1}{1}$, which equals 1.

70. D: As x goes to positive or negative infinity, only the leading term of a polynomial function of x matters. Therefore, we can ignore the "$+2$" in the denominator; $\lim\limits_{x \to -\infty} \frac{4x^2}{x+2} = \lim\limits_{x \to -\infty} \frac{4x^2}{x} = \lim\limits_{x \to -\infty} 4x$. As x goes to negative infinity, $4x$ decreases without bound. The expression therefore has no limit.

71. A: Evaluation of the expression for an x-value of -2 gives: $(3(-2)^3 - 6(-2)^2 + 4)$, which equals -44.

72. B: The situation may be modeled with the equation $\frac{1}{3} + \frac{1}{2} = \frac{1}{t}$, which simplifies to $\frac{5}{6} = \frac{1}{t}$. Thus, $t = \frac{6}{5}$. If working together, it will take them 1.2 hours to decorate the cake.

73. A: The situation may be modeled by the inequality $3x + 2y \geq 20$. Isolating the y-term gives $2y \geq -3x + 20$. Solving for y gives $y \geq -\frac{3}{2}x + 10$. Thus, the y-intercept will be 10, the line will be solid, and a test point of $(0, 0)$ indicates the shading should occur above the line.

74. C: The situation may be modeled by the following system of inequalities: $\begin{array}{l} 6x + 3y \leq 75 \\ x + y \leq 30 \end{array}$. A test point of $(0, 0)$ indicates shading should occur below the blue line and below the red line. The overlapped shading occurs below the blue line. Thus, graph C represents the correct combinations of items that she may buy, given her budget.

75. D: The table represents part of a geometric sequence, with a common ratio of 2, so it also represents points of an exponential function.

Measurement and Geometry

76. B: The following proportion may be written and solved for x: $\frac{5,280}{1} = \frac{6,700}{x}$. Thus, $x \approx 1.27$.

77. C: The volume of a cylinder may be calculated using the formula $V = \pi r^2 h$, where r represents the radius and h represents the height. Substituting 1.5 for r and 3 for h gives $V = \pi(1.5)^2(3)$, which simplifies to $V \approx 21.2$.

78. B: The volume of a sphere may be calculated using the formula $V = \frac{4}{3}\pi r^3$, where r represents the radius. Substituting 3.5 for r gives $V = \frac{4}{3}\pi(3.5)^3$, which simplifies to $V \approx 179.6$.

79. C: The surface area of a rectangular prism may be calculated using the formula $SA = 2lw + 2wh + 2hl$. Substituting the dimensions of 14 inches, 6 inches, and 8 inches gives $SA = 2(14)(6) + 2(6)(8) + 2(8)(14)$. Thus, the surface area is 488 square inches.

80. C: The volume of a pyramid may be calculated using the formula $V = \frac{1}{3}Bh$, where B represents the area of the base and h represents the height. Since the base is a square, the area of the base is equal to 6^2, or 36 square inches. Substituting 36 for B and 9 for h gives $V = \frac{1}{3}(36)(9)$, which simplifies to $V = 108$.

81. C: The surface area of a sphere may be calculated using the formula $SA = 4\pi r^2$. Substituting 9 for r gives $SA = 4\pi(9)^2$, which simplifies to $SA \approx 1017.36$. So the surface area of the ball is approximately 1017.36 square inches. There are twelve inches in a foot, so there are $12^2 = 144$ square inches in a square foot. In order to convert this measurement to square feet, then, the following proportion may be written and solved for x: $\frac{1}{144} = \frac{x}{1017.36}$. So $x \approx 7.07$. He needs approximately 7.07 square feet of wrapping paper.

82. D: The volume of a prism may be calculated using the formula $V = Bh$, where B represents the area of the base and h represents the height of the prism. The area of each triangular base is represented by $A = \frac{1}{2}(9)(12)$. So the area of each base is equal to 54 square centimeters. Substituting 54 for the area of the base and 15 for the height of the prism gives $V = (54)(15)$ or $V = 810$. The volume of the prism is 810 cm^3.

83. B: Since the figures are similar, the following proportion may be written and solved for x: $\frac{6}{4} = \frac{8}{x}$. Thus, $x = \frac{32}{6}$ or $5\frac{1}{3}$.

84. C: $\angle g$ and $\angle c$ are alternate exterior angles. Thus, they are congruent.

85. D: The corresponding angles have congruent angle measures, each measuring 44°. According to the Corresponding Angles Converse Theorem, two lines are parallel if a transversal, intersecting the lines, forms congruent corresponding angles.

86. C: The measure of the inscribed angle is half of the measure of the intercepted arc. Since the intercepted arc measures 110°, the inscribed angle is equal to $\frac{110°}{2}$ or 55°.

87. B: The following proportion may be written and solved for x: $\frac{15}{5} = \frac{6}{x}$. Solving for x gives $x = 2$. Thus, the shadow cast by the man is 2 feet in length.

88. C: The following equation may be written and solved for x: $\sin 40° = \frac{x}{6}$. Multiplying both sides of the equation by 6 gives: $6 \times \sin 40° = x$, or $x \approx 3.9$.

89. D: The area of the square is equal to $(30)^2$, or 900 square centimeters. The area of the circle is equal to $\pi(15)^2$, or approximately 707 square centimeters. The area of the shaded region is equal to the difference of the area of the square and the area of the circle, or 900 cm^2 − 707 cm^2, which equals 193 cm^2. So the area of the shaded region is about 193 cm^2.

90. B: Two of the angles, plus one side, not included between the angles, are congruent to the corresponding angles and side of the other triangle. Thus, the AAS (Angle-Angle-Side) Theorem may be used to prove the congruence of the triangles.

91. D: The Pythagorean Theorem may be used to find the diagonal distance from the top of his head to the base of the shadow. The following equation may be written and solved for c: $5.8^2 + 6.2^2 = c^2$. Thus, $c \approx 8.5$. The distance is approximately 8.5 ft.

92. D: The cross-section of a cylinder will never be a triangle.

93. D: The measure of an angle formed by intersecting chords inside a circle is equal to one-half of the sum of the measures of the intercepted arcs. Thus, $x = \frac{1}{2}(48° + 62°)$, or 55°.

94. D: The measure of the angle formed by the chord and the tangent is equal to one-half of the measure of the intercepted arc. Since the measure of the angle is 68°, the measure of the intercepted arc may be found by writing $68° = \frac{1}{2}x$. Dividing both sides of the equation by $\frac{1}{2}$ gives $x = 136°$. The measure of the intercepted arc may also be found by multiplying 68° by 2. Thus, the value of x is 136°.

95. A: The net of a triangular prism has three rectangular faces and two triangular faces. This is true of both A and C, but net C cannot be folded into a triangular prism, because the two rectangular faces on the end cannot be made to join each other. So only A can be folded into a triangular prism.

96. B: The relationship between number of faces, edges, and vertices is represented by Euler's Formula, $E = F + V - 2$. Substituting 9 for E and 6 for V gives: $9 = F + 6 - 2$, which simplifies to $9 = F + 4$. Thus, $F = 5$.

97. C: When two parallel lines are cut by a transversal, the consecutive angles formed inside the lines are supplementary.

98. B: The two triangles are similar because they each have an angle measuring 65°, and the measurement of ∠A is the same for both triangles, due to the Reflexive Property. So the two triangles are similar according to the AA (Angle-Angle) Similarity Postulate.

99. C: The triangle was reflected across the x-axis. When reflecting across the x-axis, the x-values of each point remain the same, but the y-values of the points will be opposites:

$$(1, 4) \rightarrow (1, -4), \qquad (5, 4) \rightarrow (5, -4), \qquad (3, 8) \rightarrow (3, -8)$$

100. A: A reflection across the x-axis results in a triangle with vertices at (2, –3), (4, –7), and (6, –3). A rotation of 270 degrees is denoted by the following: $(a, b) \rightarrow (b, -a)$. Thus, rotating the reflected triangle by 270 degrees will result in a figure with vertices at (–3, –2), (–7, –4), and (–3, –6). The transformed triangle indeed has these coordinates as its vertices.

101. C: The midpoint may be calculated by using the formula $m = \left(\frac{x_1+x_2}{2}, \frac{y_1+y_2}{2}\right)$. Thus, the midpoint of the line segment shown may be written as $m = \left(\frac{1+8}{2}, \frac{2+8}{2}\right)$, which simplifies to $m = (4.5, 5)$.

102. C: The distance may be calculated using the distance formula, $d = \sqrt{(x_2 - x_1)^2 + (y_2 - y_1)^2}$. Substituting the given coordinates, the following equation may be written:

$$d = \sqrt{\left(4 - (-8)\right)^2 + (3 - 6)^2}$$
$$d = \sqrt{153}$$

103. B: The perimeter is equal to the sum of the lengths of the two bases, 2 and 6 units, and the diagonal distances of the other two sides. Using the distance formula, each side length may be represented as $d = \sqrt{20} = 2\sqrt{5}$. Thus, the sum of the two sides is equal to $2\sqrt{20}$, or $4\sqrt{5}$. The whole perimeter is equal to $8 + 4\sqrt{5}$.

104. C: The area of a trapezoid may be calculated using the formula, $A = \frac{1}{2}(b_1 + b_2)h$. Thus, the area of the trapezoid is represented as $A = \frac{1}{2}(4 + 2)(2)$, which simplifies to $A = 6$. The area of the triangle is represented as $A = \frac{1}{2}(4)(3)$, which also simplifies to $A = 6$. Thus, the total area is 12 square units.

105. D: The larger triangle has a base length of 3 units and a height of 3 units. The smaller triangle has a base length of 2 units and a height of 2 units. Thus, the dimensions of the larger triangle were multiplied by a scale factor of $\frac{2}{3}$. Note that $3 \times \left(\frac{2}{3}\right) = 2$.

106. A: The vertical line of symmetry is represented by an equation of the form $x = a$. The horizontal line of symmetry is represented by an equation of the form $y = a$. One line of symmetry occurs at $x = -4$. The other line of symmetry occurs at $y = 6$.

107. C: Equilateral triangles and regular hexagons may tessellate a plane. Each triangle may be attached to each side of a hexagon, leaving no gaps in the plane.

108. A: The amount to be administered may be written as $\frac{1}{12} \times \frac{34}{10}$, which equals $\frac{17}{60}$. Thus, she should administer $\frac{17}{60}$ fluid ounces of medicine.

109. C: The slope may be written as $m = \frac{4-0}{-3-(-4)}$, which simplifies to $m = 4$.

110. D: The perimeter of the triangle is equal to the sum of the side lengths. The length of the longer diagonal side may be represented as $d = \sqrt{(4 - 1)^2 + (5 - 2)^2}$, which simplifies to $d = \sqrt{18}$. The length of the shorter diagonal side may be represented as $d = \sqrt{(6 - 4)^2 + (2 - 5)^2}$, which simplifies to $d = \sqrt{13}$. The base length is 5 units. Thus, the perimeter is equal to $5 + \sqrt{18} + \sqrt{13}$, which is approximately 12.85 units. Since each unit represents 5 miles, the total distance she will have walked is equal to the product of 12.85 and 5, or approximately 64 miles.

111. C: The following proportion may be written and solved for x: $\frac{144}{1} = \frac{2012}{x}$. $144x = 2012$. Dividing both sides of the equation by 144 gives $x \approx 13.97$. Thus, 2,012 square inches is approximately equal to 13.97 square feet.

112. D: The triangle is a 45-45-90 right triangle. Thus, if each leg is represented by x, the hypotenuse is represented by $x\sqrt{2}$. Thus, the hypotenuse is equal to $8\sqrt{2}$ cm.

Statistics, Probability, and Discrete Mathematics

113. A: Data sets B and C are asymmetrical: data set B is skewed toward lower values, and data set C is skewed toward higher values. This makes the mean a poor measure of center. Data set D is mostly symmetrical, but has a large outlier. The mean is very sensitive to outliers, and is not an appropriate measure of center for data sets that include them. Data set A is roughly symmetrical and has no outliers; the mean would be an appropriate measure of center here.

114. C: A z-score may be calculated using the formula $z = \frac{X-\mu}{\sigma}$. Substituting the score of 82, class average of 87, and class standard deviation of 2 into the formula gives: $z = \frac{82-87}{2}$, which simplifies to $z = -2.5$. Thus, the student's score is 2.5 standard deviations below the mean.

115. D: The z-score is written as $z = \frac{61-81}{10}$, which simplifies to $z = -2$. A z-score with an absolute value of 2 shows a mean to z area of 0.4772. Subtracting this area from 0.5 gives 0.0228, or 2.28%.

116. D: The z-score is written as $z = \frac{96-84}{4}$, which simplifies to $z = 3$. A z-score of 3 shows a mean to z area of 0.4987. Adding 0.5 to this area gives 0.9987, or 99.87%.

117. D: Two z-scores should be calculated, one for each student's score. The first z-score may be written as $z = \frac{68-80}{8}$, which simplifies to $z = -1.5$. The second z-score may be written as $z = \frac{84-80}{8}$, which simplifies to $z = 0.5$. The percentage of students scoring between these two scores is equal to the sum of the two mean to z areas. A z-score with an absolute value of 1.5 shows a mean to z area of 0.4332. A z-score of 0.5 shows a mean to z area of 0.1915. The sum of these two areas is 0.6247, or 62.47%.

118. D: A two-sample t-test should be used. Entering the sample mean, sample standard deviation, and sample size of each group into a graphing calculator reveals a p-value that is less than 0.05, so a significant difference between the groups may be declared.

119. C: A t-test should be used. A t-score may be calculated using the formula $t = \frac{\bar{X}-\mu}{\frac{s}{\sqrt{n}}}$. Substituting the sample mean, population mean, sample standard deviation, and sample size into the formula gives $t = \frac{19.8-20}{\frac{0.2}{\sqrt{30}}}$, which simplifies to $t \approx -5.48$. For degrees of freedom of 29, any t-value greater than 3.659 will have a p-value less than 0.001. Thus, there is a significant difference between what the manufacturer claims and the actual amount included in each bottle. The claim is likely false, due to a p-value less than 0.01.

120. B: A z-test may be used, since the population standard deviation is known. A z-score may be calculated using the formula $z = \frac{\bar{X}-\mu}{\frac{\sigma}{\sqrt{n}}}$. Substituting the sample mean, population mean, population standard deviation, and sample size into the formula gives $z = \frac{17.9-18}{\frac{0.3}{\sqrt{25}}}$, which simplifies to $z \approx -1.67$. The p-value is approximately 0.1, which is greater than 0.05. Thus, there does not appear to be a significant difference between what the manufacturer claims and the actual number of ounces found in each container. The claim is likely true, due to a p-value greater than 0.05.

121. B: A t-test should be used. A t-score may be calculated using the formula $t = \frac{\bar{X}-\mu}{\frac{s}{\sqrt{n}}}$. Substituting the sample mean, population mean, sample standard deviation, and sample size into the formula gives $t = \frac{83-82}{\frac{2}{\sqrt{30}}}$, which simplifies to $t \approx 2.74$. For degrees of freedom of 29, the p-value is approximately 0.01. Thus, there is a significant difference between what the professor claimed to be the final exam average and what the actual sample average showed. His claim is likely false, as evidenced by a p-value less than 0.05.

122. C: Use of an intact group is called a convenience sample. Such a sample increases sampling error, since randomization was not employed. The other described techniques utilize random sampling.

123. C: A z-score of 2 has a mean to z area of 0.4772, or 47.72%. Twice this percentage is about 95%.

124. D: The standard deviation is equal to the square root of the ratio of the sum of the squares of the deviation of each score from the mean to the square root of the difference of n and 1. The mean of the data set is 7.625. The deviations are −4.625, −3.625, −3.625, −2.625, −1.625, 4.375, 4.375, and 7.375. The sum of the squares of the deviations may be written as:

$$21.39 + 13.14 + 13.14 + 6.89 + 2.64 + 19.14 + 19.14 + 54.39 = 149.87$$

Division of this sum by $n − 1 = 7$ gives 21.41. The square root of this quotient is approximately 4.6.

125. A: The ends of Data Set A are farther apart, indicating a larger range. The horizontal line in the middle of a boxplot represents the median, so Data Set A also has a larger median.

126. A: The median of the lower half of the scores is 6. The median of the upper half of the scores is 16. The interquartile range is equal to the difference in the first and third quartiles. Thus, the interquartile range is 10.

127. B: The points may be entered into a graphing calculator or Excel spreadsheet to find the least-squares regression line. This line is approximately $y = 22x + 6$. Substituting 20 for x gives $y = 22(20) + 6$, or $y = 446$. Thus, $446 is a good estimate for the earnings received after 20 hours of work. If a line of best fit is predicted visually, the slope between points near that line is around 20, and the line passes near the origin. Thus, another good estimate would be $400. The estimate of $446 is closer to $400 than any of the other choices.

128. B: The mean is pulled towards the tail of a skewed distribution. It is not pulled towards the area with the larger frequency of scores. Outliers pull the mean towards those outliers.

129. C: The probability may be written as $P(M \text{ or } G) = P(M) + P(G) − P(M \text{ and } G)$. Substituting the probabilities, the following may be written: $P(M \text{ or } G) = \frac{4985}{10,079} + \frac{4113}{10,079} − \frac{2045}{10,079}$, which simplifies to $P(M \text{ or } G) = \frac{7053}{10,079}$ or approximately 70%.

130. D: The number of outcomes in the event is 2 (rolling a 5 or 6), and the sample space is 6 (numbers 1 – 6). Thus, the probability may be written as $\frac{2}{6}$, which simplifies to $\frac{1}{3}$.

131. B: The probability may be written as $P(E \text{ and } H) = P(E) \times P(H)$. Substituting the probability of each event gives $(E \text{ and } H) = \frac{1}{2} \times \frac{1}{2}$, which simplifies to $\frac{1}{4}$.

132. C: Since they are not mutually exclusive events, the probability may be written as $P(P \text{ or } T) = P(P) + P(T) − P(P \text{ and } T)$. Because the events are independent, $P(P \text{ and } T) = P(P) \times P(T)$. Substituting the probability of each event gives $(P \text{ or } T) = \frac{1}{2} + \frac{1}{2} − \left(\frac{1}{2} \times \frac{1}{2}\right)$, or 3/4.

133. B: Since they are not mutually exclusive events, the probability may be written as $P(4 \text{ or } E) = P(4) + P(E) − P(4 \text{ and } E)$. Substituting the probability of each event gives $(4 \text{ or } E) = \frac{1}{6} + \frac{1}{2} − \frac{1}{6}$, or $\frac{1}{2}$.

134. C: The theoretical probability is $\frac{1}{2}$, and $\frac{1}{2}(300) = 150$.

135. C: The number of ways the letters can be arranged may be represented as $\frac{6!}{2!2!2!}$, which equals 90.

136. A: This situation describes a permutation, since order matters. The formula for calculating a combination is $P(n, r) = \frac{n!}{(n-r)!}$. This situation may be represented as $P(6,3) = \frac{6!}{(6-3)!}$, which equals 120.

137. D: Since there are 10 numerals, the answer is equal to 10!, or 3,628,800.

138. A: The series is an infinite geometric series. The sum may be calculated using the formula $S = \frac{a}{1-r}$, where a represents the value of the first term and r represents the common ratio. Substituting 1 for a and $\frac{1}{2}$ for r gives $S = \frac{1}{1-\frac{1}{2}}$ or 2.

139. C: The number in the sample space is equal to the number of possible outcomes for one coin toss, 2, raised to the power of the number of coin tosses, or 4. $2^4 = 16$.

140. A: A Venn diagram such as the one shown below may be drawn to assist in finding the answer.

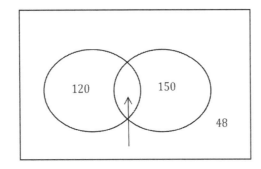

Since the set contains 320 total people, the solution is equal to $320 - (120 + 150 + 48)$ or 2 people.

141. A: $A \cap B$ means "A intersect B," or the elements that are common to both sets. "A intersect B" represents "A and B," that is, an element is in the intersection of A and B if it is in A *and* it is in B. The elements 2, 5, and 8 are common to both sets.

142. B: $A \cup B$ means "A union B," or all of the elements in either of the two sets. "A union B" represents "A or B," that is, an element is in the union of A and B if it is in A *or* it is in B. The elements in sets A and B are 9, 4, –3, 8, 6, 0, –4, and 2.

143. D: The intersection of the two sets is empty, denoted by the symbol, $\emptyset$. There are not any elements common to both sets.

144. D: If the statement is written in the form $p \rightarrow q$, then the contrapositive is represented as $\neg q \rightarrow \neg p$. Thus, the contrapositive should read, "If I do not go to the beach, then I do not get paid."

145. B: If the statement is written in the form $p \rightarrow q$, then the converse is represented as $q \rightarrow p$. Thus, the converse should read, "If it is winter, then I go skiing."

146. D: Only when both p and q are false is the union of p and q false.

147. A: Both p and q must be true in order for the intersection to be true.

148. C: A conditional statement $p \rightarrow q$ and its contrapositive $\neg q \rightarrow \neg p$ are logically equivalent because of the identical values in a truth table. See below.

p	q	$\neg p$	$\neg q$	$p \rightarrow q$	$\neg q \rightarrow \neg p$
T	T	F	F	T	T
T	F	F	T	F	F
F	T	T	F	T	T
F	F	T	T	T	T

149. C: This is a counting problem. The possible number of meals is equal to the product of the possibilities for each category. The product of 4, 5, and 3 is 60. Thus, there are 60 meals that he may create.

150. B: A tautology will show all true values in a truth table column. Look at the table below:

p	q	$\neg p$	$\neg q$	$p \vee \neg p$	$p \wedge \neg p$	$p \vee \neg q$	$p \vee q$
T	T	F	F	T	F	T	T
T	F	F	T	T	F	T	T
F	T	T	F	T	F	F	T
F	F	T	T	T	F	T	F

Only the statement $p \vee \neg p$ shows all T's in the column.

Constructed Response

1A. First, according to the problem, c is the value of the vehicle after its initial depreciation. The vehicle's value drops by 15%, so:

$$c = \$32{,}000 - (0.15) \times (\$32{,}000) = \$27{,}200$$

Using this value for c and substituting it in, the value formula then becomes:

$$y = \$27{,}200 - (0.09) \times (\$27{,}200) \times (x)$$

Finally, solve for y when $x = 2$:

$$y = \$27{,}200 - (0.09) \times (\$27{,}200) \times (2)$$

$$y = \$27{,}200 - \$4896$$

$$y = \mathbf{\$22{,}304}$$

1B. The graph of y will be linear since x is raised to the first power. Reordering the function to the $y = mx + b$ format, the y-intercept and slope are readily identifiable:

$$y = \$27{,}200 - \left(\frac{\$2{,}448}{year}\right) \times (x)$$

$$y = -\left(\frac{\$2{,}448}{year}\right) \times (x) + \$27{,}200$$

Thus, the slope is −$2448 per year and the *y*-intercept is $27,200. Plotting this function looks like the following.

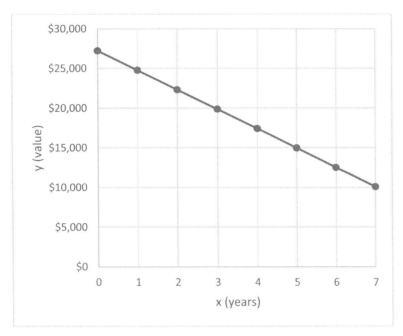

1C. Using the axis values, it is readily apparent that the value function approaches $15,000 when *x* is around **5 years**.

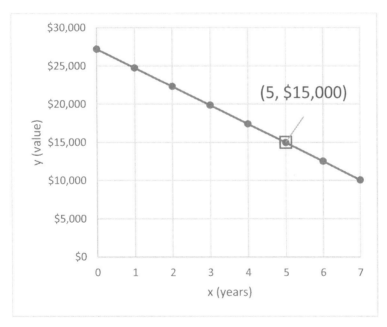

1D. The way to use the function to find when the value is $15,000 is to substitute it in for *y* and solve for *x*:

$$\$15{,}000 = \$27{,}200 - \left(\frac{\$2{,}448}{year}\right) \times (x)$$

$$-\$12{,}200 = -\left(\frac{\$2{,}448}{year}\right) \times (x)$$

$$\frac{-\$12{,}200}{-\left(\frac{\$2{,}448}{year}\right)} = x$$

$$x = 4.984 \ years$$

After rounding to the tenths place: $x = 5.0 \ years$

2A. The splash/fountain area is in the 3 circles only. To find the area, first find the radius of the circles: $r = \frac{d}{2} = \frac{6ft}{2} = 3ft$. Thus, the area for the splash/fountains is given by:

$$A_{splash} = 3 \times \pi \times r^2$$

Using $\pi \cong 3.14$:

$$A_{splash} \cong 3 \times 3.14 \times (3ft)^2$$

$$\boldsymbol{A_{splash} \cong 84.78ft^2}$$

2B. The first step in finding the percent walkway area is to find the height of the triangle, since the area is known to be $\frac{1}{2} base \times height$. An equilateral triangle has equal side lengths and equal angles of 60°. Thus, we know that the base is 30ft and the height can be found by $h = 30ft \times \sin(60°)$.

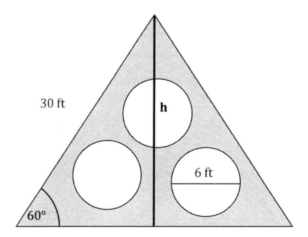

$h = 30ft \times \sin(60°) = 30ft \times \frac{\sqrt{3}}{2}$, so $h \cong 30ft \times \frac{1.73}{2}$. Thus, $height \cong 25.95ft$. Using this to find the area of the triangle minus the area of the circular splash/fountain sections will give us the total walking area:

$$A_{triangle} = \frac{1}{2} base \times height$$

$$A_{triangle} \cong \frac{1}{2}(30ft) \times (25.95ft) \cong 389.25ft^2$$

$$A_{walkway} = A_{triangle} - A_{splash}$$

$$A_{walkway} \cong (389.25ft^2) - (84.78ft^2)$$

$$A_{walkway} \cong 304.47ft^2$$

The percent walkway area is found by:

$$walkway\% = \frac{A_{walkway}}{A_{triangle}} \times 100\%$$

$$walkway\% \cong \frac{304.47ft^2}{389.25ft^2} \times 100\%$$

$$\boldsymbol{walkway\% \cong 78.2\%}$$

2C. It can be assumed that a ball would have an equal chance of landing anywhere in the area of the triangle. Thus, the probability it will land in a splash/fountain area is given by:

$$P_{splash} = \frac{A_{splash}}{A_{triangle}}, \text{ so } \boldsymbol{P_{splash}} \cong \frac{84.78ft^2}{389.25ft^2} \cong \boldsymbol{0.218}$$

3A. The median of a list of values is the centermost value of an ordered list. If the ordered list has an even number of members, then the median is the average of the two centermost values. The range of a list is the difference of the highest value and the lowest value. Thus, for this problem, the **median is 63cm and the range is 73cm − 48cm = 25cm.**

3B. The mean of a list of values is the sum of all the members of the list divided by the number of members in the list: mean =

$$\frac{48 + 53 + 53 + 54 + 55 + 56 + 59 + 60 + 60 + 63 + 63 + 63 + 64 + 65 + 66 + 67 + 69 + 71 + 73}{19}$$

Thus, **mean = 61.2 cm**

3C. The stem and leaf plot would look like this:

$$
\begin{array}{c|ccccccccc}
4 & 8 \\
5 & 3 & 3 & 4 & 5 & 6 & 9 \\
6 & 0 & 0 & 3 & 3 & 3 & 4 & 5 & 6 & 7 & 9 \\
7 & 1 & 3 \\
\end{array}
$$

How to Overcome Test Anxiety

Just the thought of taking a test is enough to make most people a little nervous. A test is an important event that can have a long-term impact on your future, so it's important to take it seriously and it's natural to feel anxious about performing well. But just because anxiety is normal, that doesn't mean that it's helpful in test taking, or that you should simply accept it as part of your life. Anxiety can have a variety of effects. These effects can be mild, like making you feel slightly nervous, or severe, like blocking your ability to focus or remember even a simple detail.

If you experience test anxiety—whether severe or mild—it's important to know how to beat it. To discover this, first you need to understand what causes test anxiety.

Causes of Test Anxiety

While we often think of anxiety as an uncontrollable emotional state, it can actually be caused by simple, practical things. One of the most common causes of test anxiety is that a person does not feel adequately prepared for their test. This feeling can be the result of many different issues such as poor study habits or lack of organization, but the most common culprit is time management. Starting to study too late, failing to organize your study time to cover all of the material, or being distracted while you study will mean that you're not well prepared for the test. This may lead to cramming the night before, which will cause you to be physically and mentally exhausted for the test. Poor time management also contributes to feelings of stress, fear, and hopelessness as you realize you are not well prepared but don't know what to do about it.

Other times, test anxiety is not related to your preparation for the test but comes from unresolved fear. This may be a past failure on a test, or poor performance on tests in general. It may come from comparing yourself to others who seem to be performing better or from the stress of living up to expectations. Anxiety may be driven by fears of the future—how failure on this test would affect your educational and career goals. These fears are often completely irrational, but they can still negatively impact your test performance.

Review Video: <u>3 Reasons You Have Test Anxiety</u>
Visit mometrix.com/academy and enter code: 428468

Elements of Test Anxiety

As mentioned earlier, test anxiety is considered to be an emotional state, but it has physical and mental components as well. Sometimes you may not even realize that you are suffering from test anxiety until you notice the physical symptoms. These can include trembling hands, rapid heartbeat, sweating, nausea, and tense muscles. Extreme anxiety may lead to fainting or vomiting. Obviously, any of these symptoms can have a negative impact on testing. It is important to recognize them as soon as they begin to occur so that you can address the problem before it damages your performance.

Review Video: 3 Ways to Tell You Have Test Anxiety
Visit mometrix.com/academy and enter code: 927847

The mental components of test anxiety include trouble focusing and inability to remember learned information. During a test, your mind is on high alert, which can help you recall information and stay focused for an extended period of time. However, anxiety interferes with your mind's natural processes, causing you to blank out, even on the questions you know well. The strain of testing during anxiety makes it difficult to stay focused, especially on a test that may take several hours. Extreme anxiety can take a huge mental toll, making it difficult not only to recall test information but even to understand the test questions or pull your thoughts together.

Review Video: How Test Anxiety Affects Memory
Visit mometrix.com/academy and enter code: 609003

Effects of Test Anxiety

Test anxiety is like a disease—if left untreated, it will get progressively worse. Anxiety leads to poor performance, and this reinforces the feelings of fear and failure, which in turn lead to poor performances on subsequent tests. It can grow from a mild nervousness to a crippling condition. If allowed to progress, test anxiety can have a big impact on your schooling, and consequently on your future.

Test anxiety can spread to other parts of your life. Anxiety on tests can become anxiety in any stressful situation, and blanking on a test can turn into panicking in a job situation. But fortunately, you don't have to let anxiety rule your testing and determine your grades. There are a number of relatively simple steps you can take to move past anxiety and function normally on a test and in the rest of life.

Review Video: How Test Anxiety Impacts Your Grades
Visit mometrix.com/academy and enter code: 939819

Physical Steps for Beating Test Anxiety

While test anxiety is a serious problem, the good news is that it can be overcome. It doesn't have to control your ability to think and remember information. While it may take time, you can begin taking steps today to beat anxiety.

Just as your first hint that you may be struggling with anxiety comes from the physical symptoms, the first step to treating it is also physical. Rest is crucial for having a clear, strong mind. If you are tired, it is much easier to give in to anxiety. But if you establish good sleep habits, your body and mind will be ready to perform optimally, without the strain of exhaustion. Additionally, sleeping well helps you to retain information better, so you're more likely to recall the answers when you see the test questions.

Getting good sleep means more than going to bed on time. It's important to allow your brain time to relax. Take study breaks from time to time so it doesn't get overworked, and don't study right before bed. Take time to rest your mind before trying to rest your body, or you may find it difficult to fall asleep.

Review Video: The Importance of Sleep for Your Brain
Visit mometrix.com/academy and enter code: 319338

Along with sleep, other aspects of physical health are important in preparing for a test. Good nutrition is vital for good brain function. Sugary foods and drinks may give a burst of energy but this burst is followed by a crash, both physically and emotionally. Instead, fuel your body with protein and vitamin-rich foods.

Also, drink plenty of water. Dehydration can lead to headaches and exhaustion, especially if your brain is already under stress from the rigors of the test. Particularly if your test is a long one, drink water during the breaks. And if possible, take an energy-boosting snack to eat between sections.

Review Video: How Diet Can Affect your Mood
Visit mometrix.com/academy and enter code: 624317

Along with sleep and diet, a third important part of physical health is exercise. Maintaining a steady workout schedule is helpful, but even taking 5-minute study breaks to walk can help get your blood pumping faster and clear your head. Exercise also releases endorphins, which contribute to a positive feeling and can help combat test anxiety.

When you nurture your physical health, you are also contributing to your mental health. If your body is healthy, your mind is much more likely to be healthy as well. So take time to rest, nourish your body with healthy food and water, and get moving as much as possible. Taking these physical steps will make you stronger and more able to take the mental steps necessary to overcome test anxiety.

Review Video: How to Stay Healthy and Prevent Test Anxiety
Visit mometrix.com/academy and enter code: 877894

Mental Steps for Beating Test Anxiety

Working on the mental side of test anxiety can be more challenging, but as with the physical side, there are clear steps you can take to overcome it. As mentioned earlier, test anxiety often stems from lack of preparation, so the obvious solution is to prepare for the test. Effective studying may be the most important weapon you have for beating test anxiety, but you can and should employ several other mental tools to combat fear.

First, boost your confidence by reminding yourself of past success—tests or projects that you aced. If you're putting as much effort into preparing for this test as you did for those, there's no reason you should expect to fail here. Work hard to prepare; then trust your preparation.

Second, surround yourself with encouraging people. It can be helpful to find a study group, but be sure that the people you're around will encourage a positive attitude. If you spend time with others who are anxious or cynical, this will only contribute to your own anxiety. Look for others who are motivated to study hard from a desire to succeed, not from a fear of failure.

Third, reward yourself. A test is physically and mentally tiring, even without anxiety, and it can be helpful to have something to look forward to. Plan an activity following the test, regardless of the outcome, such as going to a movie or getting ice cream.

When you are taking the test, if you find yourself beginning to feel anxious, remind yourself that you know the material. Visualize successfully completing the test. Then take a few deep, relaxing breaths and return to it. Work through the questions carefully but with confidence, knowing that you are capable of succeeding.

Developing a healthy mental approach to test taking will also aid in other areas of life. Test anxiety affects more than just the actual test—it can be damaging to your mental health and even contribute to depression. It's important to beat test anxiety before it becomes a problem for more than testing.

Review Video: <u>Test Anxiety and Depression</u>
Visit mometrix.com/academy and enter code: 904704

Study Strategy

Being prepared for the test is necessary to combat anxiety, but what does being prepared look like? You may study for hours on end and still not feel prepared. What you need is a strategy for test prep. The next few pages outline our recommended steps to help you plan out and conquer the challenge of preparation.

STEP 1: SCOPE OUT THE TEST

Learn everything you can about the format (multiple choice, essay, etc.) and what will be on the test. Gather any study materials, course outlines, or sample exams that may be available. Not only will this help you to prepare, but knowing what to expect can help to alleviate test anxiety.

STEP 2: MAP OUT THE MATERIAL

Look through the textbook or study guide and make note of how many chapters or sections it has. Then divide these over the time you have. For example, if a book has 15 chapters and you have five days to study, you need to cover three chapters each day. Even better, if you have the time, leave an extra day at the end for overall review after you have gone through the material in depth.

If time is limited, you may need to prioritize the material. Look through it and make note of which sections you think you already have a good grasp on, and which need review. While you are studying, skim quickly through the familiar sections and take more time on the challenging parts. Write out your plan so you don't get lost as you go. Having a written plan also helps you feel more in control of the study, so anxiety is less likely to arise from feeling overwhelmed at the amount to cover.

STEP 3: GATHER YOUR TOOLS

Decide what study method works best for you. Do you prefer to highlight in the book as you study and then go back over the highlighted portions? Or do you type out notes of the important information? Or is it helpful to make flashcards that you can carry with you? Assemble the pens, index cards, highlighters, post-it notes, and any other materials you may need so you won't be distracted by getting up to find things while you study.

If you're having a hard time retaining the information or organizing your notes, experiment with different methods. For example, try color-coding by subject with colored pens, highlighters, or post-it notes. If you learn better by hearing, try recording yourself reading your notes so you can listen while in the car, working out, or simply sitting at your desk. Ask a friend to quiz you from your flashcards, or try teaching someone the material to solidify it in your mind.

STEP 4: CREATE YOUR ENVIRONMENT

It's important to avoid distractions while you study. This includes both the obvious distractions like visitors and the subtle distractions like an uncomfortable chair (or a too-comfortable couch that makes you want to fall asleep). Set up the best study environment possible: good lighting and a comfortable work area. If background music helps you focus, you may want to turn it on, but otherwise keep the room quiet. If you are using a computer to take notes, be sure you don't have any other windows open, especially applications like social media, games, or anything else that could distract you. Silence your phone and turn off notifications. Be sure to keep water close by so you stay hydrated while you study (but avoid unhealthy drinks and snacks).

Also, take into account the best time of day to study. Are you freshest first thing in the morning? Try to set aside some time then to work through the material. Is your mind clearer in the afternoon or evening? Schedule your study session then. Another method is to study at the same time of day that you will take the test, so that your brain gets used to working on the material at that time and will be ready to focus at test time.

STEP 5: STUDY!

Once you have done all the study preparation, it's time to settle into the actual studying. Sit down, take a few moments to settle your mind so you can focus, and begin to follow your study plan. Don't give in to distractions or let yourself procrastinate. This is your time to prepare so you'll be ready to fearlessly approach the test. Make the most of the time and stay focused.

Of course, you don't want to burn out. If you study too long you may find that you're not retaining the information very well. Take regular study breaks. For example, taking five minutes out of every hour to walk briskly, breathing deeply and swinging your arms, can help your mind stay fresh.

As you get to the end of each chapter or section, it's a good idea to do a quick review. Remind yourself of what you learned and work on any difficult parts. When you feel that you've mastered the material, move on to the next part. At the end of your study session, briefly skim through your notes again.

But while review is helpful, cramming last minute is NOT. If at all possible, work ahead so that you won't need to fit all your study into the last day. Cramming overloads your brain with more information than it can process and retain, and your tired mind may struggle to recall even previously learned information when it is overwhelmed with last-minute study. Also, the urgent nature of cramming and the stress placed on your brain contribute to anxiety. You'll be more likely to go to the test feeling unprepared and having trouble thinking clearly.

So don't cram, and don't stay up late before the test, even just to review your notes at a leisurely pace. Your brain needs rest more than it needs to go over the information again. In fact, plan to finish your studies by noon or early afternoon the day before the test. Give your brain the rest of the day to relax or focus on other things, and get a good night's sleep. Then you will be fresh for the test and better able to recall what you've studied.

STEP 6: TAKE A PRACTICE TEST

Many courses offer sample tests, either online or in the study materials. This is an excellent resource to check whether you have mastered the material, as well as to prepare for the test format and environment.

Check the test format ahead of time: the number of questions, the type (multiple choice, free response, etc.), and the time limit. Then create a plan for working through them. For example, if you have 30 minutes to take a 60-question test, your limit is 30 seconds per question. Spend less time on the questions you know well so that you can take more time on the difficult ones.

If you have time to take several practice tests, take the first one open book, with no time limit. Work through the questions at your own pace and make sure you fully understand them. Gradually work up to taking a test under test conditions: sit at a desk with all study materials put away and set a timer. Pace yourself to make sure you finish the test with time to spare and go back to check your answers if you have time.

After each test, check your answers. On the questions you missed, be sure you understand why you missed them. Did you misread the question (tests can use tricky wording)? Did you forget the information? Or was it something you hadn't learned? Go back and study any shaky areas that the practice tests reveal.

Taking these tests not only helps with your grade, but also aids in combating test anxiety. If you're already used to the test conditions, you're less likely to worry about it, and working through tests until you're scoring well gives you a confidence boost. Go through the practice tests until you feel comfortable, and then you can go into the test knowing that you're ready for it.

Test Tips

On test day, you should be confident, knowing that you've prepared well and are ready to answer the questions. But aside from preparation, there are several test day strategies you can employ to maximize your performance.

First, as stated before, get a good night's sleep the night before the test (and for several nights before that, if possible). Go into the test with a fresh, alert mind rather than staying up late to study.

Try not to change too much about your normal routine on the day of the test. It's important to eat a nutritious breakfast, but if you normally don't eat breakfast at all, consider eating just a protein bar. If you're a coffee drinker, go ahead and have your normal coffee. Just make sure you time it so that the caffeine doesn't wear off right in the middle of your test. Avoid sugary beverages, and drink enough water to stay hydrated but not so much that you need a restroom break 10 minutes into the test. If your test isn't first thing in the morning, consider going for a walk or doing a light workout before the test to get your blood flowing.

Allow yourself enough time to get ready, and leave for the test with plenty of time to spare so you won't have the anxiety of scrambling to arrive in time. Another reason to be early is to select a good seat. It's helpful to sit away from doors and windows, which can be distracting. Find a good seat, get out your supplies, and settle your mind before the test begins.

When the test begins, start by going over the instructions carefully, even if you already know what to expect. Make sure you avoid any careless mistakes by following the directions.

Then begin working through the questions, pacing yourself as you've practiced. If you're not sure on an answer, don't spend too much time on it, and don't let it shake your confidence. Either skip it and come back later, or eliminate as many wrong answers as possible and guess among the remaining ones. Don't dwell on these questions as you continue—put them out of your mind and focus on what lies ahead.

Be sure to read all of the answer choices, even if you're sure the first one is the right answer. Sometimes you'll find a better one if you keep reading. But don't second-guess yourself if you do immediately know the answer. Your gut instinct is usually right. Don't let test anxiety rob you of the information you know.

If you have time at the end of the test (and if the test format allows), go back and review your answers. Be cautious about changing any, since your first instinct tends to be correct, but make sure you didn't misread any of the questions or accidentally mark the wrong answer choice. Look over any you skipped and make an educated guess.

At the end, leave the test feeling confident. You've done your best, so don't waste time worrying about your performance or wishing you could change anything. Instead, celebrate the successful

completion of this test. And finally, use this test to learn how to deal with anxiety even better next time.

Important Qualification

Not all anxiety is created equal. If your test anxiety is causing major issues in your life beyond the classroom or testing center, or if you are experiencing troubling physical symptoms related to your anxiety, it may be a sign of a serious physiological or psychological condition. If this sounds like your situation, we strongly encourage you to seek professional help.

Thank You

We at Mometrix would like to extend our heartfelt thanks to you, our friend and patron, for allowing us to play a part in your journey. It is a privilege to serve people from all walks of life who are unified in their commitment to building the best future they can for themselves.

The preparation you devote to these important testing milestones may be the most valuable educational opportunity you have for making a real difference in your life. We encourage you to put your heart into it—that feeling of succeeding, overcoming, and yes, conquering will be well worth the hours you've invested.

We want to hear your story, your struggles and your successes, and if you see any opportunities for us to improve our materials so we can help others even more effectively in the future, please share that with us as well. **The team at Mometrix would be absolutely thrilled to hear from you!** So please, send us an email (support@mometrix.com) and let's stay in touch.

> **If you'd like some additional help, check out these other resources we offer for your exam:**
> http://MometrixFlashcards.com/FTCE